Stop Smoking
Stay Cool

Stop Smoking Stay Cool

A dedicated smoker's guide to not smoking

by Richard Craze

Editor Roni Jay

Viva Books

New Delhi | Mumbai | Chennai | Kolkata | Bangalore | Hyderabad | Kochi | Guwahati

First Indian Edition 2010

VIVA BOOKS PRIVATE LIMITED

- 4737/23 Ansari Road, Daryaganj, New Delhi 110 002
  E-mail: vivadelhi@vivagroupindia.net, Tel. 42242200
- 76, Service Industries, Shirvane, Sector 1, Nerul, Navi Mumbai 400 706
  E-mail: vivamumbai@vivagroupindia.net, Tel. 27721273, 27721274
- Jamals Fazal Chambers, 26 Greams Road, Chennai 600 006
  E-mail: vivachennai@vivagroupindia.net, Tel. 28290304, 28294241
- B-103, Jindal Towers, 21/1A/3 Darga Road, Kolkata 700 017
  E-mail: vivakolkata@vivagroupindia.net, Tel. 22836381, 22816713
- 7, Sovereign Park Apartments, 56-58, K. R. Road, Basavanagudi, Bangalore 560 004
  E-mail: vivabangalore@vivagroupindia.net, Tel. 26607409, 26607410
- 101-102 Mughal Marc Apartments, 3-4-637 to 641, Narayanguda, Hyderabad 500 029
  E-mail: vivahyderabad@vivagroupindia.net, Tel. 27564481, 27564482
- Beevi Towers, First Floor, SRM Road, Kaloor, Kochi 682 018, Kerala
  E-mail: vivakochi@vivagroupindia.net, Tel: 0484-2403055, 2403056
- 232, GNB Road, Beside UCO Bank, Silpukhuri, Guwahati 781 003
  E-mail: vivaguwahati@vivagroupindia.net, Tel: 0361-2666386

www.vivagroupindia.com

Published by arrangement with

Crimson Publishing,
a division of Crimson Business Ltd
Westminster House, Kew Road
Richmond, Surrey TW9 2ND

ISBN : 978-81-309-1490-9

Published by Vinod Vasishtha for Viva Books Private Limited, 4737/23, Ansari Road, Daryaganj, New Delhi - 110 002.

Printed and bound by Raj Press, R-3, Inderpuri, New Delhi - 110 012.

This book is dedicated to my late brother Michael who didn't die of a smoking related illness.

What people have said about this book…

Damn you!! I never wanted to give up smoking before, and now you've gone and made me think of quitting. *Louise, incorrigible smoker of 22 years (up to now)*

Put this book in your pipe and smoke it. *Mike, smoker of 25 years*

This book talks to all of us who have mused on the matter of their own addiction. Profoundly insightful, I found it often struck far too close-to-home for comfort. It both amused and irritated me like a grain of sand in a pearl or one of those songs you can't get out of your head. My own Voice went into 'motormouth mode' about why I should pay no heed to it! *Charlie, consistent on-and-off smoker*

Reading this book is almost as enjoyable as smoking. *Tim, lifelong lover of tobacco, recently divorced (again!)*

I didn't have time to put it down, I was too busy reading it. The Voice spoke to me loud and clear. I heard it and have still given up smoking but please don't tell my friends. *Rob, 45, lifelong smoker*

Health Warning: This book could seriously damage your wealth. *BJ Cunningham, the merchant of Death*

This book had me laughing all the way to the tobacconist. I have kept it on the bookshelf and will certainly read it again if I ever try to quit for good. *David, aged 28, occasional smoker*

I took Richard Craze's new book, shredded it, dried it, rolled it up and smoked it. I can think of no greater accolade for a literary work. *Mark, random smoker, 42*

Thanks, now I feel seedy every time I smoke a cigarette because Leslie Phillips is stalking me as well. *Eleanor, young smoker, now given up after realising she's not as committed a smoker as Richard Craze:* If you're not going to do it properly then there's no point doing it at all.

If Eleanor's given up then I have to as well – I'm not buying my own. People shouldn't write such dangerous books. *Eleanor's boyfriend Tom, now also an ex-smoker, reluctantly*

My Voice is winning at the moment, but it is a comfort to have Richard Craze as a companion through the battle of giving up. *Elie, lapsing not smoker*

You bastard, I gave up 10 years ago but after reading Chapter 3 I'm back on forty a day and loving it!!!! *Pete, 10 year not smoker*

After reading this book, I've decided to quit smoking again. I figure if Richard Craze can do it, then so can I! Thanks for being such a special role model for me. *Mike, past previous ex smoker*

I wish I'd had this book when the Voice was saying to me 'Go on – have one, it'll make you feel better.' The book would have made me feel better about not feeling better. *Rachael, 34, not smoking smoker*

If you are a non-smoker, who has ever lost patience with smokers, then read it and you might discover that smokers aren't pariahs, polluters, irresponsible wafters of little white WMDs, inhabitors of the only carriage on a commuter train where you can ever get a seat. If you are a smoker or an ex-smoker then you know what he is saying. *Stop Smoking, Stay Cool* is full of warmth, insight and humour. *Toby, sympathetic non-smoker*

Richard Craze's book is more addictive than twenty Rothmans. *Sarah, nicotine stained smoker who now thinks she might have found an answer. It might not be the answer but it's an answer.*

Fancy giving up? Then ditch the patches and glue a copy of *Stop Smoking, Stay Cool* on to your back, today! *Tania, smoker, druggy, hip chick*

I tried smoking as a kid, a teenager and in my twenties, but never got the hang of it. Here's a guy who can *really* smoke. What a man! *Phil, 32, bad smoker*

Introduction

"It's 106 miles to Chicago, we've got a full tank of gas, half a pack of cigarettes, it's dark, and we're wearing sunglasses. Hit it."

Blues Brothers

I know. I know. There's you thinking I'm not a proper smoker. I always thought the same thing. You buy a book about giving up smoking and you think this could never have been written by a proper smoker like me. Well, let's get a few things straight. Firstly, this isn't a book about *you* giving up smoking. This is a book about *me* giving up smoking. As to whether or not you give up, I couldn't give a toss. If you want to, and this helps, good. If it doesn't, well, I never said it would.

Secondly, I *am* a proper smoker. I am more a smoker than anyone else will ever be. I am more a smoker than anyone else has ever been. I am Mr Smoking Man. I drew my first delightful lung cooling wonderful drag aged six. I was caned at school for having five Weights (a brand called Weights sold in a packet containing only five cigarettes, obviously aimed directly at the under-11s' market) in my back pocket aged 10. Or rather there were only three left in the packet hence the cane for having smoked at least two of them. At 12 I was smoking 10 a day, every day. I have smoked butts from the ashtray, smoked fags down so low I have had to use a pin to hold them, and dried out fag ends that I'd put out in a can of beer. You realise, of course, that I only did this when I was out of tobacco – you have to have some pride, you know.

I have lived and breathed smoke all my adult life. I have praised its virtues and encouraged others often and willingly. I have always despised non-smokers. I have torn down no smoking signs wherever I've gone. I once seriously considered going to live in France because their attitude to smokers is so much more grown up than ours – and when I say seriously I mean seriously to the point where I was in France looking at properties.

I have got up in the night for a fag regularly for many years being unable to go the whole sleepy eight hours without one.

As I smoked each one I was already looking forward to the next. In restaurants I order what is quickest to eat not tastiest so that I can be smoking again faster. While smoking a roll-up I have been known to be rolling the next one so I can light up again immediately the one I am smoking is finished. I've been known to have two on the go at once. I have smoked throughout respiratory tract infections, flu, bronchitis, sore throats, infections, colds, viruses, illnesses and bugs. After major surgery – appendicitis etc – I have smoked immediately I came round from the general anaesthetic. I have hidden in the toilets in hospital so I could smoke while still attached to my drip.

I have smoked where it said not to, on planes, trains, buses, in stations, airports, taxis, shops, restaurants, pubs, hotels, lifts, you name it and I've smoked there. *And* at my mother's cremation, her last big puff. She died of lung cancer due to her smoking. I am Mr Smoking Man indeed.

I have smoked not only after sex but before and, when I could get away with it, during. I have smoked in the rain, in the bath, even in the shower. I have smoked while cooking, working, driving, shaving, reading, watching telly and eating. My last gasp before going to sleep was the last puff of a fag. My first gasp as I bump-started my lungs each morning was a fag before I had got out of bed, before I had opened my eyes, before the last dream had faded, before I was even conscious.

Don't tell me I'm not a proper smoker. I make ordinary smokers look like school children behind the bike sheds having their first puff. I am Mr Smoking Man. Or rather was. I am not smoking now. This is why and how.

Chapter 1

Day 1

"If there isn't a population problem, why is the government putting cancer in the cigarettes?"

Unknown

Today I stopped smoking. Just like that. It was that easy. Well, not quite like that. And not quite that easy. How did this happen? By watching a nature programme of course. Doesn't everyone give up by watching TV? Seriously, I was watching a nature programme called *Weird Nature.* In it they were looking at some strange frogs from the Florida swamps. These frogs are a sort of mutation – they have five limbs, usually an extra back leg. This leg looks right but it hangs down uselessly. Scientists at first thought it was a genetic fault caused by chemicals or radiation or pollution. They investigated a little further and found out that they had uncovered a very bizarre life cycle indeed.

The extra leg is caused by a parasite. Its life cycle is as follows: it swims in the water of the swamp where it latches onto tadpoles. It burrows into the tadpole and waits. When the tadpole begins to change into a little froglet the parasite affects or causes some-how the mutation and makes the frog develop this extra useless limb.

Next the frogs hop about but are slower than other, more normal, frogs which makes them easier for herons to catch. They swallow the frogs. In the heron's gut the parasite lays its eggs and these get excreted out with the heron shit.

In the shit, which sinks into the waters of the swamps, are the eggs which get eaten, in turn, by swamp snails. As the eggs pass through the gut of the snails they hatch out into little swimming parasites. As the snails shit them out they begin to swim around looking for tadpoles to latch onto.

So what has this got to do with giving up smoking? Well, I'm coming to that. I'm watching this nature programme on TV and smoking at the same time. I looked at the cigarette and it suddenly dawns on me. Tobacco is just another parasite with a bizarre breeding cycle. I am just the host for it. The more I smoke, the more it gets planted. A successful crop trading its strange pleasure for increased growth. This is no more bizarre than deformed frogs/herons/shit/snails/shit/tadpoles. I look at the cigarette I am smoking and I put it out. My thoughts are: "Oh no you don't. Not again. I won't be a deformed frog for anything."

It is at that moment that I first hear the Voice. It seems to be literally screaming in my head:

Oh no you don't. I won't let you off that lightly. Roll another fag now while you've still got the chance. I won't punish you for this insurrection if you light up again immediately.

I have rebelled and the Voice doesn't like it. I am intrigued. I listen as it rants at me. I realise that I have heard this Voice before and always believed it was my own mind. But what if it is an outside force? What if tobacco is a parasite? What if not listening to the Voice helps me give it up? Surely after 40 odd years, and more doomed attempts than I care to remember, this is worth a try?

I am stunned that I have resolved to give it up and I haven't even thought about it. I have stubbed out the last cigarette and I didn't finish it. Always in the past I have finished that last cigarette prior to giving up. But the fact that I finished it in some sort of ritual meant I was actually doomed from the start. This time I don't finish that last one. I begin my giving up half way through – as if I didn't want it. Wow, this, for me, is a breakthrough.

Smoking my last cigarette in some sort of ritual always meant I was actually doomed from the start

There is a business tip that says when you make a list write down something you've already done as the first thing on the list. Then you can cross it out and feel you're on your way already. Therefore I am calling this Day 1. I know it is the evening of the first day and I haven't really gone a whole day but who cares. This is my accounting system. Tomorrow I shall call Day 2 and feel as if I have already overcome the hurdle of the first day. Clever, huh? Of course it is. If I can fool myself for 40 years that smoking is good for you then I can fool myself with this little white lie. The Voice is unimpressed, however:

So much simpler just to have a cigarette. Dear boy, you must be very stressed if you have resorted to lying to yourself, talking to yourself. Sit down and have a cup of tea and a nice soothing fag. You'll feel better and will be able to stop this nonsense.

Leave me alone.

Day 2

"I thought I couldn't afford to take her out and smoke as well. So I gave up cigarettes. Then I took her out and one day I looked at her and thought: 'Oh well,' and I went back to smoking again, and that was better."

Benny Hill

I woke up with absolutely no memory that I wasn't smoking. I went downstairs and began searching for fags. Then I remembered. The last packet of tobacco plus papers plus lighter were on the mantelpiece where I had left them. I had also left a little slip of paper with one word written on it – PARASITE. Then I remembered and went to make some tea. This, for me, was a bold move. I don't think I've ever managed to start the day without bump-starting my lungs with a fag first thing. It is only because we have a three month old baby in the bedroom with us that I don't smoke first thing in bed.

I sit here drinking my tea and looking at this computer screen. I have no idea where this is going. I hear the Voice; it murmurs seductively in my ear:

Cigarettes are your punctuation points. Without them you are just one long continuous flow. Imagine the rest of your life with no breaks. How do you think that would be?

I ignore the Voice as best I can. This is my first morning without a cigarette and it feels very strange indeed. But, and this is important I think, I have been leading up to this point for a long time now. For ages I have been unconsciously practising for just this moment. I have spent the last few months catching myself without a cigarette and saying to myself: "You're not smoking now and you're doing fine". The thought has often been enough to trigger off the instant and overwhelming craving for a cigarette. And I've often had one of course. But, and this is the important bit, I often haven't. I have observed myself not smoking and then continued to not smoke for quite a while afterwards. So this morning I am just saying to myself: "See, you're not smoking, just like all those other times."

I have spent the last few months catching myself without a cigarette and saying to myself: "You're not smoking now and you're doing fine"

When I want to I can smoke again. But right now, this moment, this here and now, I am not smoking. I refuse to look even five minutes into the future. Right now I am not smoking and that is good enough for me. I am still a smoker. I haven't turned my back on it. I am merely not smoking at this moment.

Somehow I get through this day without really thinking about not smoking. The Voice is absent as if sulking and I go to bed strangely quiet, strangely not smoking.

Day 3

"One thousand Americans stop smoking every day – by dying."

Unknown

I wake up early. I have been dreaming of smoking. I dreamt I was smoking a roll-up. When I wake up I am so relieved it was a dream. I am pleased I am not smoking. This is very strange for me. Instantly the Voice kicks in:

See, you've gone all peculiar. Probably light-headed without a fag. Better have one now. Best to start the day with a little hit.

I ignore the Voice, which has started to sound like Leslie Phillips.

Oh, I say, that's a bit beastly and quite unfair.

I know that if I am going to kick this I have to know and understand why I smoke. I know that I think/feel that smoking is cool. Grown ups smoke. Movie stars smoke. Heroes and cowboys smoke. Humphrey Bogart smoked. And it's really no use telling me that Humphrey died of cancer of the throat caused by his smoking. There is still the feeling there that he saw it through to the end. He didn't give up. Giving up is for wimps and sissies. There's the Voice again:

That's right, Champ, you smoke and be a hero, be a real man.

My first proper cigarette was at the age of eight. When I say proper I may not have smoked it properly but it was a real cigarette – Players Navy Cut with the picture on the packet of a sailor with HMS Hero on his hatband – see where the hero stuff comes from? I stole this wonderful untipped cigarette from my mother. Now she was a real smoker. I've seen her smoke 80 a day lighting each one from the dying embers of the last. We all stole her fags, her six children. She had so many she couldn't keep track of them – cigs and kids. She used to get us to light them for her off the gas cooker in the kitchen. If you just stuck a fag in the flame it didn't light properly; much better to take a drag and get it going really well.

I know that if I am going to kick this I have to know and understand why I smoke

By the age of 10 I had graduated to stealing the money from on top of the gas meter to buy five Weights – a cheaper lowlier version of the Players. I would say the gas had gone and I had put the shilling in. Then, later, when the gas did go my mother would fish another shilling out and moan about someone leaving the gas fire on too long. My sister and I did get caught once. My mother threatened us with a hand written sign made out of cardboard which said THIS CHILD IS A THIEF. I wasn't sure who was supposed to wear it or whether we should take it in turns. My sister refused to wear it and my mother said she was phoning the police. I saw her dial three numbers which I took to be 999; I was scared. My sister whispered to me that she, our mother, had probably only dialled TIM, the time – 846. My mother caught her whispering and knew she'd been rumbled. She slapped my sister, hard, and that was the end of that. The missing shilling from on top of the gas meter was never mentioned again, nor was the cardboard sign. So my sister got punished and I carried on stealing the shilling and smoking.

From five Weights I moved on to tipped Gold Flake. These were bought in packs of 10 in a wonderful red carton. I had moved up to senior school and every Monday morning was given five shillings for my lunch money. Naturally I spent it all exclusively, delightfully, selfishly, indulgently on fags. Enough to last me all the week if I eked them out. Twenty fags was about 1/11d – slightly less than 10 pence in today's money. For five bob you could buy about 50 cigarettes. Eked at 10 a day this was your fag ration for the week – assuming you could steal fags off your mother at the weekend.

You could also supplement this by 'bumming' fags off other boys. No, this had nothing to do with offering one's bottom in exchange for fags but was merely a term for cadging or wheedling cigarettes from other boys. Younger boys might well provide fags in exchange for not being hit or teased. The demon tobacco had made a criminal of me at a very early age and I regret not a moment of it.

I do remember my first proper smoking session. I was 13 and away for a weekend cadet camp at Haslemere. I had cadged enough money off my mother for the weekend to allow me the extravagance of buying my own Players. I had a pack of 10. These were to last me, eked of course, for the whole two days plus Friday evening. Most of the lads I was with decided to go into town on Friday evening but I stayed in camp. I lay on my bunk with its single grey army blanket and I smoked the first of my Players. I had heard about inhaling properly and I was resolved to try it. With the first drag I sucked as much smoke into my lungs as I could. Now everyone knows that at this point you cough your ring up and feel dizzy, sick, light-headed, disorientated and the like. Not a bit of it. Not one sodding unpleasant side effect to put me off. Instead a warm and rather mellow glow spreads throughout my entire body and I feel as if I have just come home after a rather long and arduous voyage. Well, in a sense it has been. It has been 13 years without this experience because I fervently believe I have been here before, and I've been a smoker before.

I heard angels sing. I felt great. I felt manly. I took another drag and experienced the same effect. It was simply brilliant. I smoked the entire cigarette this way. Not a single wisp of smoke was allowed to escape. I sucked it all in and blew out nothing. I absorbed that smoke. I digested it. I was the smoke. I finished the cigarette and lit another. I smoked that. And another. And another. And another. I smoked five, one after the other inhaling every microscopic trace of smoke of every drag. I felt absolutely sodding brilliant. I stood up and promptly passed out. I hit the floor semi-conscious and rolled under the bunk. Here I lay inanely grinning. It was if I had just had sex for the first time. I felt euphoric and wonderful. I knew then I was a committed smoker and that it was going to be an affectionate friend for the rest of my life.

Day 4

"Remember, if you smoke after sex you're doing it too fast."

Woody Allen

I have tried to write down all of the reasons why I smoke. But there are so many. Instead I have become obsessed with oral hygiene. My mouth feels really strange, a stranger's mouth. I have developed mouth ulcers. My tongue is sore and covered in white fur. I never had this before. Obviously the nicotine was killing all the germs. Now I am infected with mouth bugs. I have a sore throat and feel rotten. I spend most of the day in bed. I don't crave a cigarette but I do crave a return to normality. I want to feel like myself again. I want to feel like a smoker. I don't like this feeling in my mouth. I go to Boots and buy mouthwash, Strepsils and aspirin. If I'm going to feel like shit then I deserve all the medication I can get. I realise that I need little pleasures to help me replace the little pleasure cigs gave me.

No way, my friend. There is simply no pleasure to replace me. Give in now and all your mouth problems will go. I never made you ill. I never gave you mouth ulcers. Smoking is such a healthy thing, it protects you from all those colds and flu non-smokers get.

My father-in-law, bless him, sends me a bottle of brandy to help me. It is a wonderful Spanish brandy called *Cardenal Mendoza*. It is 42% proof and tastes like toffee, liquid caramel, fluid nectar. I resolve to drink one large one each evening before bed to help knock me out and assist the sleep thing. I am having a bit of trouble as I lie there listening to the Voice and thinking about cigs, a lot. The brandy does the trick and I am asleep instantly. What a lovely present, Tony, thank you.

For the first night since I gave up I sleep deeply and don't dream. I wake the next morning feeling refreshed and unable to believe that I have got to Day 5 already. I constantly remind myself that tobacco is a parasite and that I am not smoking now. I leave little notes to myself propped up in front of my computer that say: YOU ARE NOT SMOKING. LISTEN TO THE VOICE.

I leave little notes to myself propped up in front of my computer that say: YOU ARE NOT SMOKING. LISTEN TO THE VOICE

Now, you might expect me not to listen but instead I do; I want to hear the nonsense it comes out with. I spoke to an American friend today and told him about the Voice and how it sounds like Leslie Phillips. He says his Voice sounds Mexican:

Hey gringo, you wanna smoke a liddle cigarillo?

Interesting. Do we all have a different Voice? Does tobacco speak individually to each of us? Does it say what it thinks will make us break?

Day 5

"Thank you for Not Smoking. Cigarette smoke is the residue of your pleasure. It contaminates the air, pollutes my hair and clothes, not to mention my lungs. This takes place without my consent. I have a pleasure, also. I like a beer now and then. The residue of my pleasure is urine. Would you be annoyed if I stood on a chair and pissed on your head and your clothes without your consent?"

Sign from Ken's Magic Shop

Today the absence of nicotine in my blood stream has really kicked in. I read that it takes 48 hours for your body to be free, but for me it is today that has been painful. Today I have been suffering agonies of withdrawal. For the non-smoker this is probably impossible to understand. But for every smoker who has ever given up and gone through this, you will understand, you will know the dreadful clawing at the back of your throat, the tightness of your lungs, the inability to think of anything else except lighting a fag. That first drag of luscious smoke taken deep down gives instant and universal relief and relaxation and pure, pure joy.

But for some strange reason, for the first time ever, I have not given in. I have heard the Voice screaming at me to have one, to light up, to roll one, to seek easy and instant relief from this pain. But I won't. I have promised myself I'll smoke the second one, the third one, any after that. But I simply won't smoke the first one. That is the only one I am refusing. I am only turning down one cigarette; big deal.

I have promised myself I'll smoke the second one, the third one, any after that. But I simply won't smoke the first one

I do suffer from arthritis, a lot. Today has been bad. Today my ankle joints have been swollen and painful as have my wrists and finger joints.

Just one cigarette, dear boy, would ease all that pain and make you feel pretty good again. Look, there's no point getting depressed about this. You're bound to fail so why not just have one to take away the pain and then, if you want, you can go right back to not smoking. I understand.

Yeah, right. I have a feeling, no evidence mind, just a feeling that the arthritis and the fags are linked. I feel that if I can go long enough without all those chemicals the arthritis might ease off a lot. I wonder if anyone has any information on this.

Day 6

"If we see you smoking we will assume you are on fire and take appropriate action."

Douglas Adams

Oh, God. I wish I hadn't looked. I feel as if I have peeped inside Pandora's Box – if you'll pardon the expression. I have had a quick look on the Internet for any evidence to link smoking with arthritis and I really wish I hadn't. It would seem that this is the latest buzz research. Only recently has the link been made, but made it has been, and in some depth. Yep, smoking and arthritis are as linked as smoking and lung cancer.

Nonsense, dear boy. It's all hype made up by those anti-smoking buggers.

Be that as it may. I was stunned by how much there is on the Internet about giving up smoking and the dangers of it. I feel that I am so newly into it that I don't, at this stage, really want to know such things as:

- Smoking furs up your arteries
- Smoking messes up your heart
- Smoking clogs up your lungs
- Smoking increases your blood pressure
- Smoking can cause lots of different cancers – lung, mouth, throat etc
- Smoke contains thousands of chemicals, most of which are poisonous
- Smoking is very, very addictive: women need to smoke only 3 cigs to be hooked and it is around 10 for men – allegedly

I did get one good laugh out of some of it. Apparently "smoking 20 cigarettes a day means that every year 150ml of tar (one coffee cup) is deposited on the lungs, shortening life by an average of five years". Interesting. One year's smoking deducts five years from your life. I have smoked for some 35 years. For each year I have lost five years. 35 x 5 = 175 years off my life which means I died somewhere around 1825. That's what we smokers find so stupid about a lot of the statistics thrown at us to make us give up – they simply don't make sense. And why should it be a coffee cup of tar? Why not just a cup? Why the link with cigarette tar and coffee?

The Voice whispers to him of how cool he is with a cigarette, how wonderfully rebellious it is to smoke and how boring he is when he has given up

My friend Tim has just sent me a T-shirt with a picture of blackened lungs on the front and the slogan 'Smoking is Cool'. Turn the T-shirt over and there is a picture of healthy lungs and the simple word 'Right' on the back. This T-shirt has come from the Body Worlds Exhibition where real human bodies are subjected to a plasticated treatment. I'm not sure I could go but Tim says "quite amazing, beautiful, confronting. I thoroughly recommend it". Tim has now gone five weeks without tobacco and says the Voice is strong and whispers to him of how cool he is with a cigarette, how wonderfully rebellious it is to smoke and how boring he is when he has given up. The Voice says pretty much the same to me although I do notice that now I have heard the Voice I am aware that it is getting quieter. It seems to be sulking.

Not sulking, dear boy. Just waiting for you to give up this silly nonsense and come on home. I don't sulk. You seem to forget who I am. I am your friend. I have always been here for you. I was here through your first marriage break up when everything else fell apart. Remember? I was here when you needed me, always. I didn't betray you. I never turned my back on you. I didn't ever let you down.

Very persuasive. I might almost give in if any of it was true. Yep, fags were there for me when I was going through a crisis and I daresay there will be quite a few of those waiting for me up front in my future but I will have to survive without tobacco. I will have to do it without a safety net. Yes, the thought is scary and I feel lonely and very, very afraid.

Day 7

"The best way to stop smoking is to just stop – no ifs, ands or butts."

Edith Zittler

First week nearly over. I don't know how I am doing this. OK. I do actually. I am getting by, by giving in to various desires. Whenever I have been getting really stressed I have been 'troubling' my dear wife. I think she finds this quite funny. She became a not smoker nearly six years ago when she was first pregnant with our eldest child. She says that she hadn't realised Tobacco had a Voice until I mentioned it and since then she has been able to hear it loud and clear even after so long – does it ever give up?

It's not a question of giving up, dear boy. It is a question of being available whenever any of you need me. I am here.

'Troubling' her is certainly relieving the stress. Not sure that sex should really be used for such a purpose. Wonder if you could get it on the National Health? Probably not; best stick to patches (not wet ones). I did try anti-smoking chewing gum once. I don't think I've ever tasted anything so vile. I would rather smoke than chew that stuff. I did smoke rather than chew. I gave up the gum in favour of a nice fag. It tasted better, much better.

I am getting by, by giving in to various desires

The other thing I am doing is 'expressing' myself. Yes, there has been a certain amount of irritability. Not as much as usual when I've given up. In fact nowhere near as much as usual because I can hear the Voice so clearly and because of this idea that tobacco is a parasite. I won't be a host and if I have to get a bit angry to free myself of the habit then so be it. In fact if I have to kill someone to be free of it, then so be it. Yes, I will commit murder rather than smoke again. There, now I have said it, are you happy now? Does that make you feel better?

You'll crack soon. You're already talking to yourself. There's no one here. Have a fag and get a grip.

Piss off. I did read the other day about a Romanian smoker who has made his own coffin out of fag packets. Neat idea. He has collected around 7,000 packets which he has glued onto a wooden structure which is nailed together. He says he only started smoking about 12 years ago (he's now a pensioner) as he always knew it was bad for you. He smokes 40 a day and saves the filters to make a pillow for the coffin. He says he wants to be buried in the coffin to warn people of the dangers of smoking. Strikes me people should be warned of the dangers of making your own coffin. Looks like people might think you're raving mad if you're not careful. I think he's actually making a coffin out of wood and merely decorating it with fag packets.

Totally different thing.

"In attempting to develop a 'safe' cigarette you are, by implication, in danger of being interpreted as accepting that the current product is 'unsafe' and this is not a position that I think we should take."

(BAT, 1986)

Chapter 2

Day 8

"The public health authorities never mention the main reason many Americans have for smoking heavily, which is that smoking is a fairly sure, fairly honourable form of suicide."

Kurt Vonnegut

So, one week behind me. Spoke to Jake today, he's a carpenter friend. He became a not smoker a little over a year ago. He says the very first time you say to yourself you've given up smoking, you're done for, doomed. That's the second it gets you again. I can relate to that. Today I feel OK but find I can't concentrate on anything. I can't think straight. I have no memory of what I did five minutes ago.

The very first time you say to yourself you've given up smoking, you're done for, doomed

Before bed last night I watched Gosford Park with Roni, my wife. I have never seen a film in which so many people smoke. And they all seemed to be smoking roll-ups. Of course they may not have been, as the film is set in pre-filter days. But everyone smoked in it and smoked while taking a bath or playing bridge or even eating cake – proper smokers indeed. Smokers today are such a pansy bunch – frightened to smoke anywhere they aren't supposed to. I have started to notice THANK YOU FOR NOT SMOKING signs everywhere.

I fail to understand why I am being thanked for not doing one specific thing but all the other things I am not doing at the same time are ignored.

THANK YOU FOR NOT EATING BEEF CURRY
THANK YOU FOR NOT SAWING WOOD
THANK YOU FOR NOT COMMITTING RITUAL MURDERS
THANK YOU FOR NOT THINKING BAD THOUGHTS
THANK YOU FOR NOT PEEING IN THE CORNERS

Why? Why be thanked for *not* doing something? The other one I've noticed is PLEASE REFRAIN FROM SMOKING. How the devil are you supposed to do that? Hold your hand away from your mouth like some demented Dr Strangelove? And who uses the word refrain any more except on such signs?

I do feel that the motivation to not smoke is terribly important. I have given up lots of times before but the motivation was not right and I went back to it, listened and believed the Voice again. Now the motivation is right it feels good. Now I have seen tobacco as a parasite it makes it much, much easier.

Careful now, dear boy, you'll be patting yourself on the back next – and then I'll have you; because you'll have me, if you see my meaning.

The motivation to not smoke is terribly important

Day 9

"Smoking kills. If you're killed, you've lost a very important part of your life."

Brooke Shields (during an interview to become spokesperson for a federal anti-smoking campaign)

Last night brought interesting but extremely stressful episodes with Jack (aged five). Consequently I feel like a bag of shit – but a not smoking bag of shit. I feel really sorry for Jack and deeply ashamed that he has to be put through this just to make me take up the habit again – which I won't of course – but tobacco doesn't yet realise that this is for keeps.

So, Jack woke at 3.00 and was hot, feverish and in great pain. I was very sympathetic but stuck to my "You need Calpol, my boy". And he stuck to his "It's disgusting and I won't take it". Seems he would rather feel rotten and make my life a misery than suffer a couple of seconds of disgusting taste – you pays yer money…

We played around with this exciting exchange until about 5.30 when, tired and exhausted, we both fell asleep. Jack fell asleep in his bed, warm, cosy, comfortable. I fell asleep in the chair, cold, uncomfortable, not cosy. I awoke around 7.00. Jack was snoring. For just a moment I wanted to kill him – or, of course, have a cigarette. I did neither but went to make tea. That first exquisite cuppa early in the morning. The sun was up and so was I. I went and sat outside in the garden. We have a raised decking area à la Alan Titchmarsh. My father-in-law calls it our 'eatery'. I guess because it has a table and we eat there.

I sat on the eatery (or should that be in the eatery, as we have a picket fence around it?) and enjoyed my tea. Or enjoyed it as much as a night with little sleep and no fags would allow me.

Jack woke up at 7.30 still complaining. Still hot and feverish. It means, of course, that he isn't going to school. This means, of course, that he will run us ragged all day. I still feel sorry for him. Tobacco puts him through all this just to make me crack, just to make me have that first one. But I won't and poor Jack has to suffer.

Day 10

"Don't fire at me about smoking. I do it because it does me good and I could not (for I have tried and tried again) do without it. In the meantime I am keeping no horse – a most real sacrifice to me. I smoke very cheap tobacco."

Charles Kingsley

Dreamt of tobacco again last night. Dreamt I was rolling a fag and I lit it and had that first puff. I immediately woke up and was so relieved not to find a fag in my mouth. But also disappointed. Surely I could have a fag in my dreams? That wouldn't hurt would it?

Spend a lot of time at local farm shop buying fruit. I find that when the craving gets bad I can eat an apple and by the time I've finished eating it I feel better. Drinking lots of water for the same reason. By the time you finish a glass of it the craving has evaporated a bit.

Also slept a lot today on the sofa. Jack not too bad and Roni looks after him while I sleep. Jack watches TV, lots of nature programmes in the same room as I'm sleeping. He doesn't seem to notice that I'm not smoking. Mind you I don't think he really noticed when I was. I never smoked near him except very occasionally outside. I'm fascinated by the fact that he has never asked me what I was doing. It's like he knows it's an unexplainable thing. He does occasionally mention 'having a smoker' in his hand if he is holding a white stick or crayon or the like.

I have three grown up children and one of them, Luke, who is now 30, used to have a pedal car, an AA one, and he would never drive it unless he had a 'smoker' in his mouth which was invariably a bit of rolled up white paper. Seems even then I was setting an example of how to drive with a fag in your mouth. But curiously he doesn't now smoke. Good boy, Luke.

Day 11

"The best way to stop smoking is to carry wet matches."

Unknown

If I can keep this up I shall start entering on a weekly rather than daily basis when something of import happens. At the moment I am getting through each day by giving in to any cravings or desires as they arise – except of course the real one, tobacco. I'm eating a lot of chocolate. Troubling Roni. Sipping the brandy before bed, although that one may have to go. The brandy is kept in my kitchen. I have a downstairs bathroom. I have to walk past the kitchen on the way to bed after using the bathroom. Can't resist nipping in for a quick nip. I'm having two or three brandies before bed now. Tony has sent more but supplies are getting low. Down to the last two bottles. Beginning to panic a bit. Need to eat more apples perhaps. Or is there anything else I could do to relieve the nicotine craving?

Of course there is, dear boy. Come on home to papa and you'll feel fine again.

I've noticed that I smell of soap. Don't like that. It can't be healthy. I'm still concerned with oral hygiene. I've noticed that my tongue is furred up – and patchy as well. Sorry if this revolts you but it is all part of what we not smokers have to go through. You too will if you smoke and intend, one day, not to. If you're a non-smoker and have never smoked then I pity you. Fancy never having experienced what all this is about.

I have an appointment at the dentist soon so I will see what he suggests about the tongue fur.

I am getting through each day by giving in to any cravings or desires as they arise – except of course the real one, tobacco

I only ever got caned twice when I was at school and that was for smoking both times. Our headmaster – Frederick Walsh – used to make us stand in front of him and breathe out if he suspected us of smoking. This was in the early sixties at Sutton County Grammar School for Boys when free milk was still being dished out. Therefore if you had a fag in the bogs at break you always drank one of these little 1/3rd of a pint bottles of milk before heading back just in case you got caught by Fred and one of his nasty breath sniffing campaigns.

I forgot twice and twice got caught – and caned of course. Once he caned me himself which didn't hurt at all but the other time he got the deputy head to do it. Now his name I forget but I can tell you that when Pink Floyd's album *The Wall* came out with their wicked cartoon of a school master they must have modelled him on our deputy head. Now he hurt. He really hurt. He enjoyed caning. He did it for fun and none of that "This is going to hurt me more than it is you, boy." Oh no, all you got from him was "I'm going to enjoy this boy, so bend over and grip the edge of the desk for all you're worth!" And then he would take a run up and you'd get all your six stripes on the one spot.

We all talked about it and decided this was positively illegal but there was no Childline in those days and you daren't shove a copy of the house magazine down your pants because if you did and got caught – and there were those who tried and did get caught – your punishment was automatically doubled, with no get out clauses or letters from your mother.

My mother did write the best note in the world for me. Now this has nothing to do with me not smoking except she was a very heavy smoker and life for her, and with her, was tricky and consequently she could be difficult and unpredictable. I complained about having to do games – probably suffering from shortness of breath even in those days – and she immediately wrote me a note. She sealed it in an envelope and told me to give it to my form master.

I duly handed it in and he opened it, read it, smirked, frowned and told me to run along. Later Fred the Head sent for me. He said I was excused games, PE (physical education), assembly, RE (Religious Education), morning prayers, cadet church parade and pretty well anything else I wanted.

I was, quite naturally, delighted. Oh, the note? My mother, and I don't know what got into her that day – maybe she just needed a ciggie and wanted me off to school as quickly as possible – had written that we were practising Buddhists and thus we couldn't compete in games nor take part in any Christian ceremonies. Bingo, it got me out of anything I didn't fancy although in later years I did play rugby for the school and no one commented on this blatant defiance of the Buddha's religious tenets.

Day 12

"A custom loathsome to the eye, hateful to the nose, harmful to the brain, dangerous to the lungs, and in the black, stinking fume thereof, nearest resembling the horrible Stygian smoke of the pit that is bottomless."

King James I, A Counterblaste to Tobacco

My worst day so far. Woke feeling OK but furred, sore throated and tasting of evil things. But I was doing OK. I was doing fine. I enjoyed my tea. I enjoyed sitting still for a while drinking it. Roni reminded me I had to go to the doctor's. Nothing serious. Quick blood test to check my cholesterol levels which have been abnormally high. I don't know if this is diet, genetic or what as I had never had the tests before about six months ago so they might have always been high.

Anyway Ruth, the nurse, took the blood and I asked if smoking could affect the levels. She said it was likely so I said I was not smoking and she said that was good. Then she threw the spanner in. She suggested that I take the breath test. I immediately breathe out milky fumes all over her thinking she wanted the old Fred Walsh test but apparently she was suggesting a completely different test altogether.

This test involved me blowing/breathing into a tube connected to a machine. It will test for lung damage. Non-smokers score 0-5. Light smokers who gave up years ago 5-10. Moderate smokers who gave up years ago 10-20. Light smokers now 20-30. Moderate smokers 30-40. Heavy smokers more than 40.

So I blew and breathed and expected a fairly high score seeing as I have only gone without a smoke for a mere 12 days.

Guess what I scored?

3.

Yep, 3.

"Why have you given up?" Asks Ruth, "You have the lungs of a non-smoker. Not someone who has given up but someone who has never smoked."

Can you imagine what this has done? Can you imagine what the Voice is chortling in my ear now? Oh yes. Oh yes.

See, dear boy. I told you I wouldn't harm you. Everything is fine. Listen to nursie, she knows best. You can now smoke with impunity knowing no harm can come to you. Imagine how unstressed you'll be. Go on, have one. Enjoy. You now know the truth. All that nonsense about damage to the lungs is just plain lies. Now you know who is telling the truth.

And on and on and on and on. Couldn't she have lied? Couldn't she have told me my lungs were scarred, bruised, damaged, shot to ribbons, pockmarked with deep craters and fissures of blackened tissue? But no, she has to say "3". Just like that. And give the Voice so much ammunition I shan't get any peace today.

Day 13

"Realistically, if our Company is to survive and prosper, over the long term, we must get our share of the youth market. In my opinion, this will require new brands tailored to the youth market."

RJ Reynolds, Research Planning Memorandum on Some Thoughts About New Brands of Cigarettes for the Youth Market, February 2, 1973

Off to see Glynn, my dentist, today. After yesterday's shock horror I really need someone telling me that I'm doing good not smoking. Glynn has moaned about stains from red wine and coffee and tobacco so often in the past he will be pleased I've given one of the deadly three up.

Glynn looks at my furry tongue and pronounces it to be a reaction to the toothpaste he recommended last time to remove the stains of tobacco, wine and coffee. I proudly tell him I am not smoking. He frowns and says "Bastard".

"What?"

"I hate people who've given up", he says.

"But you've always told me off about the stains."

"Yes, but I never told you to give up, just get rid of the stains. Which is why I suggested the tooth whitening toothpaste last time. There's no need to give up, no one likes an ex-smoker, you know. They're all smug bastards. No one likes a smart arse."

He cleans my teeth in grim silence and I notice for the first time the very faint aroma of tobacco around him. Bastard himself. Still my sense of smell seems to be getting better.

The Voice casually mentions:

See, if professionals such as your dentist smoke then it must be OK. Now he must see incidents of mouth cancer all the time and he still smokes which tells you that smoking and mouth cancer are unrelated. He knows the truth. He is part of the great conspiracy. Professionals know that smoking is not only not harmful but positively beneficial. He wouldn't smoke if it wasn't. Go on, have one and join the ranks of the wise and clever, the secret clan of professionals who know the truth. Go on, just the one.

I ignore it.

Day 14

"Much smoking kills live men and cures dead swine."

George D. Prentice

If I can get through today I will have not smoked for two weeks. But I am not smoking now, at this moment. There is no "I've given it up", or "I'm a non-smoker now". All I am prepared to say is "I am not smoking". I don't qualify that in any way. I am just not smoking. I could have just put one out. I might be about to light one in a few minutes. But now, this moment, right now I am not smoking. That's what is getting me through. Just this moment. No other. There is no need to look ahead or back. Just this one moment.

All I am prepared to say is "I am not smoking"

I sure could do with a cigarette. It would be nice as I feel panicky without tobacco. I feel my security and props have been taken away. I can't think properly. I can't work. I can't sleep. I feel rotten, tired, lethargic, depressed. Roni says I am doing well. She says I seem very calm. I tell her that what is outside and what is inside are obviously two very different things. Roni says she would be surprised if I went back to it. I say I wouldn't, it's much too early for her to be making predictions like that. I miss it. I am a smoker. I miss the pleasure. I have cut out a major pleasure centre of my life. Smoking is very, very pleasurable and I miss it dreadfully.

So smoke again my young friend. There is nothing worth suffering so much for. You've proved your point. You can live without me now. You know it. I know it. You've beaten the addiction. Now you could have one and relieve the stress and not have to smoke again full time. You could just have one when you fancied. You've got me beat. I accept defeat. You've proved yourself the stronger.

I am driving back from the dentist's when I see a packet of tobacco lying in the road.

It's a sign. Stop! Quickly. There. It's what you've been waiting for. Stop!

I find myself braking, slowing down. Is this a sign? Has this tobacco been left here for me? Should I stop and go back and swoop this up into my arms and thank God I have been saved? Is it a sign?

Yes, yes, Stop! Go back! Go back!

I drive on. It is not a sign. It is a packet of tobacco that someone has carelessly, litter-ally thrown away. It is not a sign. I order Gollum out of the car. He, of course, won't go.

You'll never know if you don't go back. It might have been full of luscious wonderful tobacco.Go back!

I drive on. I'll never know if it was full or empty but it was not a sign. There are no signs.

Now we all know that Raleigh brought tobacco back from the Americas but where did the Indians get it from? Well, I've done a little research and it seems that the North American Indians got it from the Mayan civilisation in Central America. They grew tobacco as a pain killer for wounds – a poultice of chewed leaves does apparently reduce inflammation and pain. Chewing it got them hooked.

The pain killing qualities are only now being investigated by scientists. It is also supposed to relieve Parkinson's disease, the pain of arthritis (interesting or what?); can be used as a poultice for bites and stings; and can be added to bath water to make a strong infusion which gives full body relief and a sedative effect. Apparently the nicotine inhibits nerve signal transmission to the brain by stimulating various inhibiting nerve pathways. Cocaine, morphine and other opiate analgesics act to give pain relief in the same way. Yep, and I bet tobacco is just as addictive a pain killer.

That's all bunkum, dear boy. Scare stories put out by killjoys. You've seen the evidence. I kill pain, not joy.

Tobacco was used by the peoples of what is now Mexico and Peru for ceremonies and medicinal purposes. They also used it to relieve the pangs of hunger during famines. Columbus is credited with introducing it to Europe, and I'm no historian so I don't know if that is still the accepted view or whether the poor old Vikings now get the blame.

Once in Europe it was spread by sailors and explorers, especially the Portuguese and Spanish, followed closely by the French and us Brits. And it was us that reintroduced it back to the Americas as a commercial cash crop. Didn't we do well? Today some one thousand million people worldwide smoke. And good luck to them. I have no problem with smokers. I might have a problem with the Voice of Tobacco and the way it slimes in my ear. And I might also have a problem with the tobacco companies. After all, they spend something like a billion dollars a year persuading poor sods like me to continue the habit. I'm not just fighting the one single cigarette but a whole raft of executives, ad men, commercials, bill boards, subliminals, and corporate shenanigans.

"The average life expectancy here is about 40 years, infant mortality is high: the health problems which some say are caused by cigarettes just won't figure as a problem here."

The Rothmans representative in Burkina Faso (1988)

Chapter 3

Day 15

"For the first time in history, sex is more dangerous than the cigarette afterward."

Jay Leno

The Voice has been busy today. It has been reminding me of how wonderful certain things are with a cigarette. For instance it has been telling me that going for a swim is better when you come out and towel yourself dry and then sit and watch the waves while smoking that after-swim cigarette. This may be true. It is something I've always done. I say always. Obviously I didn't when I was five but even then I did feel I was missing something.

When I was a kid we lived in Brixton – Mother's voice: "Don't say Brixton, darling, say Tulse Hill, it sounds so much better" – very close to Brockwell Park swimming pool. We, six kids, all learnt to swim there. My mother would swim almost every day in the summer if the weather was good enough (open air swimming pool) and always had a fag when she came out. As a small boy I would watch her desperate to emulate her and have one myself.

So, what happens when you next go on holiday? You know the wonderful feeling of having that fag after your swim in the sea. You'll crack then. You won't be able to enjoy anything any more, especially that swim. Why not have a cigarette now, willingly, consciously, positively, rather than cracking on holiday and thinking yourself a failure? If you have one now by choice isn't that better?

This Voice is so sneaky. Its logic is impeccable, believable, convincing, persuasive. Unfortunately it is real but wrong. Brilliant but flawed. Plausible, but unconvincing this time around. I have given in to this Voice so many times before. Now I see the parasitic quality I am stronger.

Or is that weaker?

No, it is stronger. I don't want to be a host to a parasite. I don't want to be played for a fool. Yes, I think and feel smoking is cool, grown up, relaxing, enjoyable and smart. But it is also life threatening, dirty, smelly, addictive, uncool, expensive and unfair on others. It is a parasite. It does prey on us to increase its own spread. It does turn us into addicts so it can be more successful. And the other hosts – other smokers – become its unwitting accomplice to help its spread. The tobacco corporation bosses are as much its victims as us, the poor smokers at the end of the chain. Tobacco's seductive Voice has been listened to by billions and all of us have been seduced and turned into hosts. It's a bit like the film *Invasion of the Body Snatchers* and we are all in the thrall of aliens who have sucked our minds out.

I do think you're being a little unfair here. I don't force myself on anyone. You all have a choice. And I'm not addictive. That is propaganda.

So how come I find it so hard not to smoke then?

Because I am so pleasurable. You'd find it as hard to give up sex, food, wine, breathing, laughing, smiling, loving, telling jokes, writing, driving, watching TV. I am not a parasite. I don't reproduce in your lungs. I don't live in you as a plant or infection. I am a gift from the gods to give you pleasure, ease your pain, help you relax, protect you from colds and chills, make you fear less and enjoy more. I am your friend.

Day 16

"The sex was so good that even the neighbours had a cigarette."

Unknown

After yesterday's discussion with the Voice it seems to have gone quiet. Good. I could do with a day off. I am thinking a lot about this parasite business. I guess it has sown the seeds of doubt. I mean, what is a parasite? And is tobacco capable of being one? I've been delving a little and found that the parasite that causes the deformities in frogs is called *Ribeiroia*, and it also causes the same trouble in lots of amphibians including Californian newts, Pacific tree frogs, bullfrogs, Western toads and Colombian spotted frogs. The snail which plays an important part in this life cycle is on the increase hence the increase in the number of deformed frogs. The increase in snail population is down to enriched fertiliser levels in ponds, rivers, lakes etc. Because of the increase in snails amphibian populations are falling. This is of concern, naturally, to conservationists.

There is another bizarre parasite life cycle I've discovered. This one is just as complex. Don't read on if you don't like gore or spiders – or wasps come to that.

There is another bizarre parasite life cycle I've discovered. This one is just as complex. Don't read on if you don't like gore or spiders – or wasps come to that

There is a parasitic wasp. Ah, you'll say, there's lots of those. Yes, but not a wasp just laying its eggs inside a caterpillar or whatever. This one is really weird. This is a Costa Rican wasp, *Hymenopimecis.* The adult wasp pretends to have got itself trapped in a spider's web. When the spider comes along to kill it, it turns the tables on the spider and stings it in the mouth. This paralyses the spider which allows the wasp to lay an egg on the arachnid's abdomen in safety. It lays its egg and flies off. When the spider recovers it goes about its normal daily doings. It is unaware that it is now a living, walking larder for a wasp larva. Once the egg hatches, the larva immediately sets about making small holes in the spider's abdomen so it can suck out its *haemolymph* (spider guts) and at the same time inject it with an anticoagulant to stop it producing quick clotting agents to seal up the holes. When the blood/guts do clot they form a large scab which the larva then clings onto – a bit like making a saddle. I told you this was going to be horrid.

Finally the larva is big enough to leave 'home'. The anticoagulant it has been injecting into the spider also contains a chemical which causes the spider's mind to warp and it begins to spin a really unusual web. This web is the larva's cocoon, inside which it will change into an adult wasp. Once the spider has spun this cocoon it dies owing to the poison in its system – a bit like freaking out after a major drugs overdose such as LSD. The larva then has a last big feast – the opposite of the condemned eating a hearty breakfast – and lets the empty body drop to the ground. It then closes the cocoon around itself and waits to emerge as a beautiful adult wasp.

Now this is a complex parasitic life cycle; it involves mind altering drugs causing the death of the host; it doesn't involve reproduction of the parasite in the host's body but it does induce a change in the host's nervous system which may or may not involve a hit on the pleasure centres; it causes changes in normal behaviour that involve carrying out a procedure that it wouldn't normally (spinning a cocoon). Does this sound like anything else we know? I think it does. I think it is just as bizarre as the life cycle of the tobacco parasite plant. Scientists in years to come will award me the Nobel Prize for my exploratory work in the field of the tobacco parasite. (I don't mean the award ceremony will actually take place on a tobacco farm… oh, forget it.) No one else has identified this yet so perhaps I could put in a little plea for a research lab to carry on my fine work. I might look at cloning next.

Day 17

"I kissed my first girl and smoked my first cigarette on the same day. I haven't had time for tobacco since."

Arturo Toscanini

Woke up in a frightful panic. My snot has turned white. Rushed downstairs clutching detritus in paper hanky to show my wife – or rather to attempt to show her. She, strangely, didn't share my enthusiasm and refused to look at it.

"But it's turned white, for God's sake."

"It's supposed to be white."

"It can't be. It looks so pallid and ill, so anaemic and... and… well, thin."

"It's supposed to look like that."

I for one preferred my proper snot; tobacco stained snot

Well, I for one preferred my proper snot; tobacco stained snot. How many more of these phenomena do I have to experience? Isn't it bad enough that I can now taste everything and that everything smells? Isn't it bad enough that all air is now fresh to me? Isn't it enough that all I can smell is soap on my hands now? If I stop hawking up brown gobby stuff in the morning then I'm taking smoking up again. My wife says everything will turn white eventually. I find that a scary thought, very scary. Everything?

Day 18

"Do you think I get up every morning and think of ways to hook kids? Don't you people have any f***ing conscience?"

CEO of RJ Reynolds

I used to comfort myself, as a smoker, with the thought that the incidence of bowel cancer among smokers is much lower than among non-smokers. I figured that if a cancer was on offer then a lung cancer might be preferable. After all you have two lungs and you might get away with the removal of one. But bowel cancer? Well, I figured you've only got one arsehole and having that removed would seriously curtail your enjoyment of life.

No arse, no morning dump, no reading the paper while other people hammer on the door demanding you come out right this minute. Instead you could wander around dumping into your little bag worn so discreetly around your waist anytime you wanted. Where's the fun in that? I do appreciate that for bowel cancer sufferers this isn't funny. It isn't funny to me. I wanted to avoid it at all costs. I smoked some more just to be on the safe side.

I did of course have a bowel cancer scare. Bleeding from the bowel is a scary thing. Very scary. I had been reading a report about looking back after you've had a dump. I looked back and saw a blood splattered bog. Very, very scary. I went for the tests. Finger up the bum. Sorry but that doesn't get me going if you know what I mean. I had to swallow some really foul stuff and have an X-ray. I was surprised to see the foul stuff again on a screen in white. As the stuff went through the bowel it exploded into curves, twists and weird tubes. One of the most bizarre things I have ever seen in my whole life. Just for a second it was almost worth being there.

Verdict? All clear. All remained clear until a couple of months later when again, looking back, saw the blood splattered bog. Panic. Then suddenly remembered all the beetroot eaten the day before. Had beetroot previously also. Again not funny. My doctor, who I confessed to, thought it very, very funny. I didn't. I smoked some more.

Day 19

"Cigarette smoking is a major cause of statistics."

Fletcher Knebel

I did give up once before – ignoring all jokes about how easy it is to give up, I do it every night, I've done it lots of times etc – for eight months. This was around 1975 and I was worried about first batch of children being born and me smoking around/near them. I have simply no memories of those eight months. None whatsoever. How did I give up? I don't remember. Why did I take it up again? Some idiot bought me a lighter for Christmas and I just had to try it out. Had the one cigarette and that was it. Next day I was back to 20 a day.

That was in the days when I smoked Benson & Hedges. Gold packet. Gold lighter (gold colour anyway). I was working in a London casino as a croupier and we all smoked Benson & Hedges or Dunhill. They were the only two smart brands. Something to do with the gold packs. Clever marketing. I have seen an Arab punter tip a valet for bringing him a pack of B&H. The amount? Oh, you really don't want to know. You do? OK. Five grand. I told you, you didn't want to know. These valets all had houses all around the world and why didn't I switch from being a lowly paid croupier to a valet? Because these valet jobs passed from father to son or were bought and sold for a lot of money. Besides which I am English and we are a proud race. What, wait on tables? Me? Never. Thus we remain poor and proud.

How did I give up? I don't remember. Why did I take it up again? Some idiot bought me a lighter for Christmas and I just had to try it out

Do you remember the Benson & Hedges ads from way back? They used to be sort of arty, interesting, eye catching, thought provoking (God, I sound like a Coca Cola advert). There was one that had a fish on a piano with its face propped up by a packet of Bensons – pun was *piano tuna.* Another had a wave, made up entirely of Panama type straw hats, clutching (if a wave can clutch) a pack of Bensons with the by-line Goodbye Gringo (7,4) as a sort of spoof crossword puzzle. The answer being of course Mexican wave. What this had to do with the fags I don't know. It didn't tell you the fags were stronger, better, smoother, had more/less nicotine/tar than other brands, gave you cancer quicker than others or what.

There was another whole series of surreal ones where packs of Benson & Hedges were disguised as other things: a pack became part of one of the pyramids or a half opened can of sardines, a mouse trap waiting outside a mouse hole and even a parrot in a cage. These ads were themselves spoofed with a pack posing as a snake crawling across the sand complete with the slogan 'Advertisers speak with forked tongue'. No idea who put that one out but I guess they didn't like the ads.

All these ads came with the relevant warnings: MIDDLE TAR DANGER: Government Health WARNING: CIGARETTES CAN SERIOUSLY DAMAGE YOUR HEALTH. I do remember my daughter having an Australian boyfriend who was aghast at these warnings. He said in Australia all it said was DON'T SMOKE IF YOU DO SPORTS or the like implying smoking might make you a bit short of breath but that was about it.

Back to the ads. Gallahers, who made Bensons, also made Silk Cut and they did a whole series of wacky ads. I never smoked Silk Cut, found them to be too weak, a pale smoke with no bite, insipid and bland. How do I know this? Of course I would smoke them if there was nothing else. Silk Cut ads usually featured some purple silk cut with scissors or a knife or a razor blade. I remember one where the purple silk was the screens round a hospital bed. You didn't see the scalpel, you didn't need to.

To build brand awareness they were brilliant. You knew a Silk Cut ad immediately. There was another one with a hand wearing a silk glove with one finger cutting off the call on an old fashioned Bakelite phone – clever, eh? – silk cut. Or how about the line of scissors can-can dancing wearing – you've guessed it – purple silk skirts. About five or six years ago the ad agency Saatchi's did a spoof Silk Cut ad showing a pack that had been crudely cut and then stitched back together again with purple silk sutures. I think they were trying to say they were back again – not the fags but the advertisers. Perhaps they did the original ads. Who knows? Who cares? We just remember the can-can dancing scissors. Who cares who did it?

I think I know who really did it, if I may be allowed to speak.

You're not.

But I did do art. I did clever ads.

You just make people smoke.

Oh no, I offer much more than that. I offer an entire lifestyle, art, identity; suave, cool sophistication. Remember when you clicked that gold Dunhill lighter as you lit a Bensons, weren't you the coolest of the cool? Those of you who smoked Bensons in your casino days, weren't you all young lions?

Yes, and how many of us are still around?

You are. You haven't died of any horrid diseases. What's your beef? What, precisely, is your problem? You made it. You're still here. How do you know the others aren't all still alive as well? You have absolutely no evidence that any of them are dead. You took to me like a duck to water. Together we were ultracool. Now you've got it into your head to turn your back on me. Well, fine. But do remember all the pleasure I gave, all the good times we had together. Don't turn me out just because you can't hack the thought of one day dying. Don't blame death on me. You are going to die anyway. Just because you have given up smoking doesn't mean you'll live forever. So why not smoke and be happy?

Good line of argument but forget it. There is nothing you can say or do that will make me have a cigarette, OK?

Don't bank on that, buddy. You won't last long without me.

But I did manage to go eight months without a fag. So I can do it. I have done it before and there is no reason why I shouldn't go just as long again – or even longer. I have promised myself that I shall smoke again when I am 90. If it shortens your life then chances are mine has already been shortened so I shouldn't lose too much. This way I can look forward to smoking again one day so I haven't given up, merely not smoking at the moment. Hey, it's whatever gets you through this process. My biggest worry is the old 'I'll put on three stone if I give up'. How fat shall I get? Answer: not much fatter than I am now. I have resolved:

- No sweets to counteract the loss of nicotine
- No nibbling on biscuits between meals
- Cut out all puddings after meals

I have also been looking at advice online to see what I'm supposed to be doing. Skipping breakfast is a bad idea apparently as it just makes you hungry. Better to eat a low fat breakfast instead. Also nibble on fruit, eat low fat yoghurts, low fat muesli bars, toast with savoury spread such as Marmite. Of course none of these even remotely appeals to the dedicated smoker. Marmite instead of a roll-up? I should cocoa.

But if I'm not smoking at the moment then I do need to watch my weight. I have stocked up with lots of nuts, dried fruit, raw vegetables such as carrots and I might try some of the sugar-free gum recommended. I am also going for lots of freshly steamed vegetables at meal times. I am trying to stock up (so to speak) on veggies so I don't keep feeling hungry.

Apparently people put on weight because they feel hungry, need to keep up some sort of oral satisfaction (I chew pens), eat more because food tastes better, replace the end of the meal fag with another helping of pudding (guilty). I did also read that smoking actually cuts down the rate at which food is absorbed in the gut so giving up means we actually digest more even while eating the same amount. This could be as much as 30%. Therefore to maintain our weight when we stop smoking we actually need to cut down the amount we eat, otherwise we pile on the pounds.

To maintain our weight when we stop smoking we actually need to cut down the amount we eat

The urge to eat crisps, chocolate and sweets only lasts a few weeks after giving up. This I read online. What nonsense. My craving for chocolate has been around as long as I've been on solids. Same with crisps. I was addicted since I first ate a packet in the cinema aged five. You used to get those crisps with the little blue bags of salt in them. I ate the crisps and then found the blue bag. Naturally I ate that as well. Ugh! But I did like the crisps and have eaten them ever since. I don't think I'm eating any more since I haven't had a fag but I shall have to watch it. I will opt for the low fat option whenever possible.

I'm also trying to steam everything rather than fry or roast. I don't take sugar in tea or coffee which is a bonus. And I'm cutting all fat off meat before cooking it. I have also tried to switch from red wine to white, cut out beer altogether (not that I ever drank much of it), am using semi-skimmed milk (skinny milk as I think of it) and I'm trying to cut out cheese as well.

Don't get me wrong, this weight thing isn't taking up too much of my time. I have enough problems avoiding all the traps and pitfalls the Voice sets me up for to devote too much to whether I'm too fat or not. I can lose weight later; I can't deal with lung cancer later.

Oh, come on. You're beginning to sound very wibbly indeed. Why not go and live in Glastonbury? Praising raw vegetables indeed. How pathetic. Have a fag and be a man. Come on, have a grown up pleasure for God's sake. Everyone knows fat people are happy and fat people who smoke are almost in heaven on earth. Next you'll be taking up exercise and wearing a headband and a Walkman. How sad you've become. I'm almost on the point of giving up on you.

Exercise? What? Oh, come on. Do I look like the sort of person to do exercise? Of course not. OK, OK, I'll walk the dogs a bit more often and for a bit further but that's it. I couldn't set foot in a gym to save my life – yes, yes, I know it might just do that. I'm allergic to lycra, all sports, gyms, exercise machines, sweat, getting out of breath, jogging, headbands, people running attached to any sort of personal music device. In short I am going to die rather than subject myself to the indignity of exercising. A gentleman simply doesn't get sweaty or out of breath or wear track suits. That's it. No further discussion. I like Noel Coward's advice – if you're fit you don't need to exercise; and if you're not, you shouldn't be doing it.

I couldn't agree more. There's no need to do anything when you could be sitting back in your chair having a nice cup of tea and a fag. Imagine, no, remember, how cosy life used to be? Just you and me and a cup of tea. There is no finer sport than relaxing with a fag.

I've just read that "scientists at the University of Bristol calculate that 11 minutes of life expectancy go up in smoke each time you light a cigarette. They say they hope these numbers will help spur tobacco smokers to join the ranks of their matchless peers". God, at least two crap puns in there at our expense. Now, if you smoke roll-ups you will know how often they go out. So you need to relight them many times – do you lose 11 minutes each and every time? Or just the first time? What if you light a cigarette and don't smoke it? Still lose 11 minutes? Now I have smoked on average 20 a day for say 40 years, therefore I have lost 11 x 20 x 365 x 40 = 3,212,000 minutes = 53,533 hours = 2,230 days = 318 weeks or a bit over 6 years.

This is a lot less – almost bearable for all the pleasure smoking gives – than the five years off for every year spent smoking figure. Also, the six years comes off the end of your life, not in the middle or the beginning. I sometimes wonder if, when you're 90, you'd miss not going to 96? I expect at 90 I shall crave life as much as I do now and would not go gentle into that goodnight. I would kick and scream just as much as I would today. I ain't going quiet.

There's no need to, dear boy. Have a fag and relax, chill out. You're not going anywhere just yet. Oh, you might be popping your clogs soon if you don't take it a bit easier. There's only so much stress you can endure.

Don't you realise tobacco was sent by the gods so you didn't have to carry the entire burden yourself. Tobacco is here as a comforter. Imagine how naked life would be without anything to ease the pain. Do you really want that?

I have to if I don't want to be the host to a parasite.

Day 20

"I phoned my dad to tell him I had stopped smoking. He called me a quitter."

Steven Pearl

As I approach the end of my first three weeks without tobacco I am questioning my identity as a not-smoking-at-the-moment-thank-you-sort-of-person. I mean, who is this new smelling of soap person I have become? When I smoked I was a smoker; that was me. I smelt of tobacco and damp corduroy. I was relaxed and chilled. I wore John Lennon glasses and read John Updike and liked a nice cup of tea (mind you I am drinking upwards of 20 cups a day now. Is that another addiction I shall have to address in time?) and walking my dogs across fields where I could lean on a gate and have a fag and watch the clouds and internally philosophise about life and death and the universe and everything.

Now I am sharp with the children, cold and fresh, smelling of carbolic, afraid to sit still for too long in case I give in to this damn ridiculous Voice in my head, unable to work or sleep, eating too much, a neurotic bundle of twitches and jerks. I mean, who am I now? Do I approve of who I have become? Am I the sort of person

I wouldn't have shared a railway carriage with before? Have I become a New Man? I liked the old me, the smelly, slightly singed around the edges me. I have become…no, I can't say it…I have become…a non-smoker. Arg!

You see, smoking is so attractive. Smoking is rebellious, young, carefree. It makes such a defiant statement about who you are. If you smoke you are signing up to wearing a leather jacket with the collar turned up, listening to rock and roll, staying up late, talking about life and everything, rebelling and behaving like a grown-up. Now you are washed and ready for bed after your tea. You are a child again. You smell nice but of nothing real or grown up or dangerous. You have gone from being James Dean to Wendy Craig in one swift stubbing out of a fag. You are a disappointment to me.

And to myself. I could almost weaken. This is such a persuasive argument. I could, almost. I do like the idea of smoking a pipe. I've always thought the smell of damp tweed and pipe tobacco a good thing. My grandfather smoked roll-ups. He had a silver tobacco tin with a sunburst engraved on it. How do I remember it so clearly? I have it by me as I write. My uncle gave it to me to remember Pop by. I used it for many years myself but it is now redundant. Pop died of emphysema/bronchitis/pneumonia due to his smoking, at the age of 68. I don't think a day goes by when I don't think of him and miss him.

I didn't have a father so my grandfather was the nearest I got to a role model/father figure. Is this why I have smoked so long, so often, so much? I have to question it. To beat this Voice I have to know why I smoked. My grandfather rolled roll-ups gently, with time and care and, as a small boy, I would watch him fascinated, hypnotised, in rapture. I loved the smell of them, of him.

Now I can remember the hawking cough which I blanked at the time and the fact that it was smoking which killed him. It also killed my mother at the age of 70. Did she smoke because her beloved dad did? Were we all trying to be like Pop? To be Pop? He was the kindest, funniest man ever. We all loved him.

> *My grandfather rolled roll-ups gently, with time and care and, as a small boy, I would watch him fascinated, hypnotised, in rapture. I loved the smell of them, of him*

Notice how the Voice goes quiet when the serious business of smoking comes up? When we talk of death and cancer and people we have loved who are not here any more because they smoked, the Voice has nothing to say. Have you noticed? Because I have and it is one of my defences against smoking again. When that urge gets almost unbearable I remember Pop; I handle his tobacco tin lovingly and understand why he isn't here, why he was missing in action so young, so stupidly, so pointlessly and I listen for what the Voice has to say and it is silent.

Smoking represents to me being grown up. When I was a kid I hated being a kid. I wanted to be grown up more than anything else. Smoking was my passport out of childhood; my ticket to the adult world. I suppose it could just as easily have been alcohol or thieving or sex. Alright it was sex too but this isn't so health risking or addictive (ha!). When I was 15 I tried to get in to see the film *Day Of The Triffids* (an X certificate – you couldn't see it if you were under 16) I pulled my collar up and stuck a fag in my mouth to look older, more grown up. The ruse didn't work. I was duly thrown out and quite right too; it really was a dreadful film as I came to realise later when I did see it. But it was the fag which I thought gave me the aura of grown-upness. Children don't smoke. Grown-ups smoke. Therefore if I don't smoke I have reverted to childhood. Mind you at my age that might not be such a bad thing.

Mike and his girlfriend Louise called in for supper last night on their way to Cornwall. It was my first real chance to sit in a room with real smokers since I've given up. I was stunned by:

- How much they smoke – and straights at that
- How they use a cigarette as a prop – to make a point, to cause a dramatic effect, pausing to light a fag just before the punchline of a story, that sort of thing
- How they would always light a cigarette before embarking on the next story
- How smelly the room seems
- How smelly the room is in the morning
- How disgusting the ashtrays look

And yet I watch them hypnotised, haunted. I watch each movement of hand holding fag, transfixed like a snake watching its prey.

I am fixated on anything to do with smoking at the moment. I watch for smoking in films, on the TV. I watch people smoking in cafés, pubs, in the street. I can smell a smoker a mile away. I watch every little gesture smokers make with their lips and hands as they indulge their vice, their passion.

On one level I am really glad I've stopped; on another I am appalled, disappointed, not understanding. It's a bit like having your head above water – dry, clear in the sunshine – while below the waterline it is all panic and confusion. I crave it constantly, every second, every day. My lungs are throbbing, my head feels heavy and pounding but I will not smoke. I won't have that first cigarette. I will have any beyond that first one, but not that first one. I am only denying myself one lousy cigarette, that first one. Saying no to only one isn't such a hard thing to do, is it?

Saying no to only one isn't such a hard thing to do, is it?

I really, really want a cigarette but I will not follow my grandfather into that smoke filled room of death, not yet, not now, not just yet.

All this talk of death does make me think that you have a quirky view about smoking and death. I do think you've got hold of the wrong end of the stick. Just because you have given up doesn't mean you are going to live forever. Let's face it, you are 52 so really what's the point of giving up now? Huh? If there is any damage to be done – and I don't believe there is – it must already be done. Imagine how you are going to feel in a few months when you go for a check up and they tell you you've got a terminal illness, how on earth are you going to cope with that without a fag? Huh? Answer me that?

Balls. I will live longer anyway.

How's that?

When I smoke I don't do up my seat belt as I need access to my pockets. Now I am not smoking I do up my seat belt. It's not the cancer that would have got me but a road traffic accident. I also drive more safely because I concentrate more; I'm not forever scrummaging around to get at baccy or papers or a light. And I can't tell you the number of times I've nearly crashed through dropping hot ash down my front or missing the window when throwing a still burning fag end away. Anyway, I'm not here to argue with you.

But I am right, aren't I? You have left it a bit late.

Late? At least I'm having a go. Look you've stopped me giving up so many times in the past with your false logic and perverted reasoning. I got so sick of you telling me I was a failure every time I broke down and took it up again that I even gave up giving up on the premise that if giving up was making me unhappy then not giving up would make me happy. You've twisted my thinking for so many years I have been brainwashed, indoctrinated and conditioned by you to such an extent that I don't even know what I think anymore. I would like a break just to clear my mind and know what is down to you addicting me, and what I really think and feel about smoking. OK?

It's entirely up to you. If you think you can do without the pleasure principle then go right ahead, be my guest. I shall only support you, comfort you and be there for you again when you come to your senses. Is that OK?

If only it were true.

Day 21

"If children don't like to be in a smoky room, they'll leave." When asked by a shareholder about infants, who can't leave a smoky room, RJ Reynolds chairman, stated, "At some point, they begin to crawl."

Carrig, David 'RJR Wins Fight', USA Today: B1, April 18, 1996

Today is three weeks. I don't want to get cocky but I shall reward myself with a small tot of the Cardenal Mendoza before bed – that's on top of the two or three I was planning to have anyway. Although I'm not celebrating in anyway I do feel good about this. I do hate it when people say "congratulations". There is nothing to be congratulated about. Each and every second of these last three weeks has been a struggle. There is no easy way to cure an addiction as strong as this.

And why should you want to, dear boy?

Because you are a parasite that sits in my brain feeding me nonsense. I want you out of my system and out of my life.

I may be changing my mind as your hold lessens. I don't know. I haven't had long enough free from you to be able to think clearly yet. And, no, that doesn't give you hope. You are not re-establishing your tentacles in my mind.

There is no easy way to cure an addiction as strong as this

Tom called round today. He's given up as well. He said he could hear the voice really clearly. He gave up because he was in New York last New Year's Eve and found he couldn't breathe properly. He wanted to be partying but couldn't get his breath right and felt quite sick. He says he has resolved not to smoke again if smoking means missing out on life. We talked about various ways we've both tried – and failed of course – to give up. I said I had tried acupuncture, hypnosis, nicotine gum, eating sweets, worry beads, the fake cigarette.

Tom has tried patches, homeopathy, herbal remedies, scare tactics (visiting a hospital to see a newly removed cancerous lung), signing an oath in blood (we've both tried this one), having bets with best friends (again both of us), smoking dope (yep), taking up running (not me!), changing brands (interesting one this, Tom swears that changing brands and smoking a different cigarette every time breaks the habit. Did it work, Tom? Of course not).

What I realised is that none of these methods worked because they weren't treating the actual tobacco habit. They were trying to treat the symptoms, if you like, and not the disease. Only by seeing tobacco as a parasite and learning not to listen to the nonsense the Voice utters am I able to begin to free myself of this dreadful addiction. Tom says pretty much the same is true for him. He says he has chosen health over pleasure. I have chosen freedom over addiction. We have both prioritised not smoking over smoking. And yes, we're both finding it hard. Who said it was going to be easy? And if we fail?

Then we fail but we will try again, and again, and again. We are both committed to freeing ourselves. We both now think of it as freeing ourselves from something horrid that has got us in its hold and we must wriggle free. It's a bit like being caught by some dreadful invisible monster with numerous tentacles, as soon as you get one arm free it grabs you with another 10 tentacles.

Will we keep it up? I hope so for both of our sakes. I miss my grandfather and don't want my kids missing me too early, too needlessly. I really would like to be around to see how they turn out.

OK, OK. If smoking really is as bad as you two have decided it is then have just one to test your theory. If you had one and could really taste how horrid it is, test how revolted you would be, how repulsive this whole smoking thing is then you'd be really free of me, wouldn't you?

Nice try but I've just realised that all the things I've done to give up smoking in the past haven't worked because I expected them to work. I thought that chewing gum or having acupuncture or patches or whatever would do all the hard work for me. Instead I now know I have to do all the work and all the giving up tactics are just a help to relieve the symptoms. Giving up has to start in the mind. If I haven't given up mentally already then no amount of homeopathy or hypnosis is going to work.

Yes, these things are really useful, valuable in helping you get over the nicotine craving, the addiction, but they don't actually give up smoking for you. That has been my mistake. I thought that was what they did, a sort of wonder cure, a magic drug or bullet that did all the hard work. No wonder they never worked. I was expecting too much of them. This is very important.

I thought that chewing gum or having acupuncture or patches or whatever would do all the hard work for me, but they don't actually give up smoking for you

One of my brothers gave up – and he was a heavy smoker – when he had to make a long haul flight to Australia. The thought of all that time without a ciggie was enough to make him realise how in the grip of addiction he was. He walked away from smoking at that point and has never gone back in 10 years. You see, he gave it up in his mind first and thus didn't need patches or gum or anything. Once he'd seen his addiction for what it was, he was free. Yes, he too had cravings and restlessness and jittery nerves and all the other symptoms we all have but he was able to work his way through them because he had already given up smoking and thus was able to look elsewhere for the relief he needed. That's what we have to do, give it up in our heads first. This is important.

But that's where I am, isn't it?

Yes, and that's where I have to confront you, to tackle my demons first. If I can't lick you in my head I shall never be free. The sweats and the jitters and the sleeplessness are all side effects. They aren't the giving up smoking. The giving up is a mental thing.

Sounds mental to me, dear boy. Why go without all that pleasure? Why put up with all those horrid symptoms when you could just have a fag and be free of them? It isn't natural to live with the jitters.

It was smoking that gave me the jitters in the first place. I have lived with the drugged state of nicotine for so long I have forgotten what it is like to be clean of it. That's why your body reacts so much, why you get the jitters – it is things returning to normal and should be welcomed not fought against. In fact the worse the jitters the faster you are getting the nicotine out of your body.

And of course it's not just the nicotine. I've been reading about additives in fags. Boy, was I gullible to think that giving up was going to be easy when you think about what they put in tobacco to make us smoke more, become more and more addicted. Some additives, apparently, are allowed, to improve the cigarettes provided they are safe. For instance to prevent the ash falling off too easily, or to control the rate of burning, or to inhibit the growth of mould. But the actual harm that these additives do hasn't really been researched.

There have been some moves to have the additives in tobacco regulated but not the ones in the filters or paper initially. But since 1984 a voluntary agreement was reached to include a ban on all additives in parts of the cigarette that are intended to be burnt. The interesting words here are 'voluntary' and 'burnt'. Thus they don't need to sign up to it, and nor does it include the filter. Glad I smoked roll-ups. But hang on – I did smoke Benson & Hedges for many, many years.

Since 1997 there has been a new directive to the cigarette manufacturers. They mustn't add any new additives to the ones already on the approved list. How many on the approved list? Oh, you don't want to know. No, you really don't. You do? My, you are a glutton for punishment. OK. *Six hundred.* Get that? Fag makers can add up to 600 additives to their product. Anybody done any research on how any of these 600 could work in conjunction with any of the others? Nope. No one is bothered. As long as we keep smoking they can keep adding. And any not on the approved list shouldn't be used… but this is only a voluntary agreement. Basically they can put anything they want in just so long as you don't actually keel over and die in the tobacconists.

The sweats and the jitters and the sleeplessness are all side effects. They aren't the giving up smoking. The giving up is a mental thing

Some of these additives include sugar and chocolate and other sweeteners so the tobacco loses it's harshness; eugenol and menthol are added to numb the throat to mask the aggravating effects of tobacco smoke; cocoa is used to dilate the airways allowing the smoke an easier and deeper passage into the lungs; and finally they add stuff to make the smoke less visible and less aromatic (smelly) to those not smoking (thus disguising the impact of passive smoking). Ah, good, you say, that should make it all better. But hang on, how much harm is done by breathing in burning sugar fumes? Or a combination of sugar fumes, tobacco smoke, addictives (sorry, I keep typing addictives instead of additives by mistake) to stop the ash falling off into your lap, burning paper and something to 'inhibit the growth of mould'? Got any idea? No? Well that's OK because nor have the manufacturers – or if they have they ain't saying.

But a spokesman for the American tobacco manufacturers says that all this additive stuff is for the American market and that UK fags don't have anything like as many additives; 90% of UK fags are additive free. Yeah.

The US State of Massachusetts is forcing tobacco companies to disclose which additives are used in which brands and why. The industry is responding by suing. John Carlisle, Director of Public Affairs for the Tobacco Manufacturers' Association, dismissed the claims as "nonsense and scaremongering". "We are doing everything that is asked of us by the government to ensure that we produce a product in which the UK consumer can have total confidence."

Mr Carlisle said that if anybody was unhappy with the additives that were legally allowable in the UK, then they should complain to the government. He would not confirm that additives were not used to increase the addictiveness of cigarettes.

Cigarettes are one of the few products – if not the only one – which when 'used as the manufacturer intends actually kill you'. I am indebted for that phrase to an acquaintance, BJ Cunningham, who used to own a wonderful cigarette company called, appropriately, Death Cigarettes. You may remember these from the nineties with their distinctive white embossed skull and crossbones logo on a two tone black background. BJ used to sponsor the Gay pride march in London under the banner 'Death Cigarettes – the Honest Fag'. God, there ain't much that man doesn't know about marketing. On the Death fag packet there was the wonderful phrase: et in Arcadia ego – even in Paradise, Death is still here. For me personally I translate this as: even in Paradise I can hear the Voice telling me it would be that little bit better if I could just have that one cigarette.

The great thing about Death Cigarettes is that if you were carrying a pack around no non-smoker was going to say "Don't you know smoking kills you?". They'd just see the pack and shut up. I smoked the tobacco for a while until BJ's company went tits up because he got hounded by the real tobacco manufacturers who wouldn't let tobacconists stock his honest fags, and also because Customs and Excise didn't like him selling cheap duty free fags from Luxembourg. Fascists. I've still got a Death Cigarette lighter – Zippo of course, silver with an engraved skull and crossbones logo. And a proper logo: a skull without an eye patch. What is that they do with skulls these days; why the eye patch? A skull hasn't got any eyes, right?

What brand you smoke says a lot about you

BJ says that what brand you smoke says a lot about you: "Bensons say 'I'm classy, gold packet, part of high society. Marlboro say I'm an outdoor type, I like wearing a cowboy hat and riding horses'. But Death Cigarettes say 'Yes, I'm killing myself, but at least I know it, and I smoke a brand which doesn't try to hide the fact'". I'm not sure what smoking Golden Virginia tobacco said about me (ex-hippie, creative type? I like to think so). My grandfather smoked Three Castles tobacco (round white tin with the three castles picked out in red – neat) and I tried some once. It must have been before additives because it took the back of my throat out. No wonder he died at 68.

BJ is another fanatic smoker. Claims he started at 11 and has smoked since. Now he is even more committed than me as he has had collapsed lungs and still smokes.

"The cigarette industry has been artfully maintaining that cigarette advertising has nothing to do with total sales. This is complete and utter nonsense. The industry knows it is nonsense. I am always amused by the suggestion that advertising, a function that has been shown to increase consumption of virtually every other product, somehow miraculously fails to work for tobacco products."

(1988) Former CEO of McCann-Erickson, which has handled miliions of dollars in tobacco industry accounts

Chapter 4

Week 4

"I'm glad I don't have to explain to a man from Mars why each day I set fire to dozens of little pieces of paper, and then put them in my mouth."

Mignon McLaughlin

So, as I begin the last week of my first month how do I feel? I have a permanent sore spot inside my nose and there's blood in my snot. My lungs feel tight and breathless. My tongue is furred. Everything tastes of fish for some strange reason. Everything still smells of soap. I'm not working as well as I would with tobacco but it does feel as if it's getting better. I'm sleeping and easing off the brandy. I'm still troubling the delectable young Roni but she's not finding it quite so funny (I think). The kids haven't noticed I'm not smoking. I don't feel like a non-smoker which is a blessed relief.

Tony, Roni's father, says that in giving up you have three days of agony, three weeks of misery, three months of wistful thinking and three years of adjustment. So, I've had my three days of agony and three weeks of misery. I look forward to three months of wistful thinking. If that's as bad as it gets I think I can cope. I would like tobacco not to be my first thought whenever things get tough. Yesterday when out driving I got cut up by a maniac in a white van (do they realise what a stereotype they are?) and as the red fog of road rage descended I immediately thought "a cigarette would help here". The Voice was suddenly helpful.

Yes, you could have a quick fag and be really chilled. Look at you, your pulse is racing, your blood pressure must be off the scale and you're quite light-headed. A fag would be the quickest and easiest way to relax.

One day my first thought won't be tobacco and I look forward to that day. I do feel healthier, or rather I'm not thinking about cancer quite so much. I must admit to being a bit of a hypochondriac when it comes to tobacco related illnesses. Every cough I ever had was cancerous and now I'm not smoking those thoughts seem to have receded which is a relief. I do still cough up great brown gobs of goo in the mornings but I now see them as my lungs rejecting the nicotine layers they must have built up instead of cancerous lumps.

One day my first thought won't be tobacco and I look forward to that day

The Voice has been laying some interesting advice at my door:

If you had a cigarette now think how delicious it would be to be smoking and no one would know. You could smoke in secret. It would be like taking a lover. Think how wonderfully wicked that would be. Imagine the secret pleasure. You could wander off down to the river and have a private fag and watch the water go by and no one would ever know but you. The longer it goes the more attractive it would be to smoke and still get the kudos of giving up. Your friends would congratulate you and you could smile smugly – and STILL BE SMOKING; how brilliant!

I do find I am focusing a lot of my anger on things which piss me off at the moment such as why I have to be given a plastic stirring stick in motorway service stations instead of a proper spoon. And why should everything come in flat packs for me to put together? All this used to be done in a factory. People are unemployed. I'm doing the job they used to do. Why do I have to be the finishing department?

And why does my toaster go up to 10 when it burns anything above a two? Why do ice cream tubs contain less on the inside than they appear to do on the outside? Who do the makers think they are kidding? I know I'm being cheated. Why are the tiles at my local swimming pool designed to be very slippery when they are wet? Pictures of food on packaging, why do we have to be so disappointed? Why do I have to have music played at me when on hold on the phone? Why so many options whenever you phone a company?

Why put sweets next to the till in shops so your kids will scream when you say no? Why inserts in magazines which fall out on the floor in the newsagents? Or at least they do when I pick up the magazine, but Roni says I do it on purpose. Why do my youngest baby's trousers have pockets in them? For God's sake he is only 11 months old, what do they think he's going to keep in these spurious pockets? Why do all videos have those long ads for other films at the beginning? No one watches them. We all fast forward.

Roni's chickens escaped this morning. Have you ever tried to round up such stupid birds? They scatter in every direction and the stress of trying to catch them was almost worth a fag. I got breathless running round the garden. I got cross. I snapped at Roni – apparently that isn't the first time I've done that since I've given up – and had to be reminded that it isn't her fault I left the chickens' gate open. Fair play.

So, I've been snapping have I? Well I'm not surprised. This isn't easy. WARNING: Giving up smoking can seriously damage your relationship. Although Roni gave up nearly six years ago when she got pregnant with our first child, Jack, and hasn't smoked since (I think this a little extreme; there must be easier ways of giving up – and more pertinent to men?), nevertheless she lusts, oh yes, she lusts after tobacco just as much as I do even after all this time. Does this addiction ever wear off? She does say she was a crap smoker and would give up if she got a cold and never smoked during the day but only in the evenings. How do they do that? Her brother is the same.

I could never have done that. I smoked from the moment I first opened my eyes to the last moment I closed them.

When I was first married – not to Roni – I had three children who are now all growed up. When this first batch was young I tried to give up and promised them £1 each if they ever saw me smoking again. Within half a day I had broken down and had to have a ciggie. Dutifully I gave them their blood money and enjoyed my fag. About half an hour later I had another one. Bliss. Then I looked down and saw three little hands open in front of me. They expected £1 every time I had a fag. I had to explain economics to them in a very loud voice.

My mother smoked so I smoked. True or false? I smoked when the first batch of children were young. They saw me smoke although I tried not to smoke around them, but outside they saw me smoking. Their mother didn't smoke and has never done so. One of them smokes like a chimney. One smokes intermittently. One doesn't smoke. So of their parents half smoked and half didn't. Of the children about half and half again. This time round if both Roni and I don't smoke we might be setting a good example and all three of this second batch might not smoke at all and that would be a good thing.

Roni says she was a crap smoker but I always thought her rather sexy when she rolled a fag. There is something incredibly delicious about a woman smoking. Faber brought out a fab book of smoking with a photo of Marlene Dietrich on the front cover smoking, wow!

When Tony, my father-in-law, gave up food he used to practise saying "No thanks, just coffee" whenever the sweet trolley put in an appearance. I've adopted the same principle with fags and when offered I say "No thanks, I've just put one out". Whether this will work indefinitely I don't know but it does save having to explain that I'm not smoking and why etc.

When offered a fag I say "No thanks, I've just put one out"

Wherever I have lived I've always had an open fire. I've tried wood burning stoves but never really got on with them. Yes, they give out as much heat, perhaps more, but they aren't for me. Or so I thought. I have just installed one as it is cleaner, safer, warmer. The reason? I don't need the open fire any more. I don't need to throw fag ends into the fireplace. Wow. This may seem nothing to you but it is a major breakthrough to me. It has been a revelation that smoking has affected my life so deeply, so intimately, so completely.

Little details like wearing a seat belt; not needing an open fire; not having to keep patting my pockets to make sure I have my tobacco, papers and lighter; not having to make sure I've got an ashtray near me; not having to look for the smoking areas in restaurants; not having to check that there aren't any children around before lighting up.

My life is changing. Things are different. I feel like I've lost a lover. It felt the same when I got divorced 15 years ago. You spend a lot of time looking for someone who isn't coming any more, and you're not quite sure how to be. My first wife and I used to start each day with a cup of tea. When I got divorced and lived on my own I didn't know what to start the day with because tea was something we had done together. It's the same with smoking. I don't know what to begin my day with.

I've just been to see Christian. He is, allegedly, a cranial osteopath. And a French one at that. Oh, I'm sure he is – osteopath I mean – and I know he is definitely French. I'm sure he is qualified too but I think he's more; somewhat of a healer. I went because he has quite a reputation; Roni goes as she has a recurrent bad back and Christian puts it right. My arthritis has been bad lately – since giving up smoking actually. Christian said my energy was all over the place and none of it is in my body. I explained about giving up smoking and he says I may well have smoked as it grounds you, keeps you in your body. If I have always suffered this disembodied energy thing then it would make sense. Sorry, make sense? I'm sounding like a Glastafarian new ager. Of course it doesn't make sense. Christian says that if he can correct the energy thing then the need to smoke should evaporate. Good pun for a Frenchie.

I had to lie down on his couch while he put his hands under my back. His hands were cold and remained thus throughout the treatment which I found very strange. Anyone else's hands would have got warm under your back. The process felt strangely calming. I fell asleep at one point. Coming out after 45 minutes I feel calm and very, very relaxed. I get home and immediately fall asleep. When I wake up I still feel calm and relaxed. Perhaps this energy thing works. I have no idea. I know nothing. Hey, whatever gets you through, huh?

I have been to acupuncturists three times for giving up smoking in the past. First time I went it was to a local doctor who had done a weekend course in acupuncture and was hopeless. He treated about 10 of us all at the same time by putting a needle in the side of our noses. One chap fainted and the doctor didn't seem to know what to do with him. Another woman had massive bleeding from her nose and again the doctor seemed at a complete loss.

Hey, whatever gets you through, huh?

The next acupuncturist was qualified properly but she didn't do a lot for me. She said my sense of smell might improve and when I came out all I could smell was dog mess in the street so I had to have a fag to kill the smell.

The third time was better. I did feel less needy about smoking for a couple of days but it wore off quickly. The third acupuncturist did Japanese acupuncture and he was really helpful in treating the arthritis but the smoking was left pretty well unaffected. Again I am sure I had to give up in my head first. These things may have helped with the symptoms of nicotine withdrawal but they couldn't give up for me.

When I went to hypnotherapy it was good and I listened to the tape afterwards but it didn't seem to help the smoking at all. I used to run a natural health clinic in Somerset many years ago and I can tell you that the hypnotherapist and the homeopath both smoked and they used to treat people for smoking. Hey, I smoked and I used to recommend either the hypnotherapist or the homeopath. I think I understand why it is called a hippocritical oath.

I thought I would read a give up smoking book to see if I was missing anything. I got so stressed reading it I nearly had a fag. What a lot of tosh. It said things like how much you hated that first cigarette. Rubbish. I loved it. How much you envy non-smokers. Again rubbish. I despise them. It says how much healthier you'll feel immediately. I feel dreadful. I can't breathe properly. My chest is tight. I can't concentrate. I can't sleep. It says your sense of taste and smell will recover at once. Yeah, but who wants to smell soap and taste fish? It says things that seemed so at odds with my own case that I wondered whether it could help anyone.

Then I thought that perhaps I am unusual as a smoker and that others are happy to be patronised and that it does help them give up. I would have rather had the truth personally. It ain't easy. Giving up smoking is a shitty thing and it hurts and it's hard. Reading a book that says it's easy – all you have to do is throw the packet away and it will be all plain sailing after that – is plainly talking through its fag packet. It's hard. It's hell and there is no cure for cold turkey. There is nothing to take away the pain, the regret, the desperate, desperate need to smoke.

We all have to WANT to want to give up

Only by treating this as a parasite have I been able to make any headway. We all have to find our own parasite. We all have *to want* to give up. We all have to want to want to give up. It's all a subtle psychology. We have to work in the mind and not in the physical. The actual smoking isn't what we are fighting but ourselves, our own inner voice, our own schizophrenic nature that partly says I hate smoking and partly says I love it. One side will always win. We have to come down on the side of the angels.

There is another side, the side of pleasure, of the devil, of rebellion, of danger, of darkness and wicked sin. I am that side, dear boy. I am your pleasure principle. I am all the things you've dreamed of and yearned for and lusted after. I am the tart in the doorway with the split skirt and the fishnets and the red lips offering untold sexual escapades and fun. I am not your mother scolding. I am your best friend, your lover, offering passion and pleasure and pain. I am fun and redemption. I am everything that has ever called to you. I am your benefactor and tormentor and seducer and companion.

Yeah, right. You are also killer and sadist, perversion and evil, disgust and failure, cancer and slime. You have killed my relatives and friends. You have distracted me from my work. You have made me smelly and disgusting. You have made me loathe myself at times and regard myself as pitiful and pathetic. Don't you see, I am better off without you?

You'll never know how much pleasure you are missing if you give up now. We were only just beginning to know each other. You were just getting the hang of it.

"A statement linking smoking to LUNG CANCER looks right to the uninitiated public. By improving the 'accuracy' of the warning without apparent need, its credibility is enhanced and I wonder whether this is really in the best interest of the industry."

Philip Morris, 1988

Chapter 5

Week 5

"What a weird thing smoking is and I can't stop it. I feel cosy, have a sense of well-being when I'm smoking, poisoning myself, killing myself slowly. Not so slowly maybe. I have all kinds of pains I don't want to know about and I know that's what they're from. But when I don't smoke I scarcely feel as if I'm living. I don't feel as if I'm living unless I'm killing myself."

Russell Hoban, Turtle Diary, 1975

It's been a good month and a lousy month. Jack's just talked about cutting down. Not his smoking, mine. I got up really early this morning to do some work in my study. Jack woke early as well and I hoiked him out so he wouldn't wake his brothers. Then I realised I had to do something with him. He had some maths homework to finish so I suggested he joined me in the study. We both worked quietly until I could hear the others stirring over the baby monitor. Jack then asked me what I was working on and I told him about this book. I explained that smoking probably wasn't a good idea but it was really hard to give it up. Jack then said "Why don't you stop slowly? Have 10 one day, nine the next, eight the next and then, before you know it, or in 10 days, you'll be smoking none at all." Brilliant! If only it was that simple but I do like the way a five year old works things out as quickly as that.

I told Roni about this later and she said I should ask Jack about the psychological problems with giving up; she thinks he may have some good advice for me. I increasingly see this whole giving up smoking thing as a series of skirmishes rather than one main battle. Turn your back on the bugger for a moment and it's back in your life and back in your lungs. If you can win enough of the little skirmishes you're on your way to winning the war. But it is a long hard slog and there is no respite; you don't get a day off from this addiction. There are no easy ways, no easy cures. You have to be alert to the dangers 24 hours a day, every day. The Voice is as likely to strike in the small hours of the morning as it is when you're offered a fag by a friend. You can't afford to relax for a moment.

I increasingly see this whole giving up smoking thing as a series of skirmishes rather than one main battle

When my mother smoked Players when I was a kid there was a wonderful bit of nonsense written on the flap of the packet. As you pushed the sliding pack open the flap was the first thing you saw and it said: *It's the tobacco that counts.* There used to be this crap joke about two men and two camels lost in the desert and one man hears 1, 2, 3, 4, and he begs his friend to stop counting. His friend says he wasn't. They continue and the counting starts again. Finally the man draws his gun and in desperation shoots his friend. The counting begins again. He eventually shoots both camels because they won't stop counting. At last just before he shoots himself he has a last smoke, opens his Players and sees: *It's the tobacco that counts.* Look, I told you it was a crap joke.

I woke up one day this month dreaming of all the brands I've ever smoked: Gauloise, Gitanes, Players, Senior Service, Black Russian, Bensons, Dunhill, Embassy (with coupons, you collected them and traded them in via a catalogue for a crap carpet sweeper. Don't mistake the coupons for Green Shield Stamps, they came with all grocery products, you collected them and stuck them into a book and when you had enough books you could trade them in via a catalogue for a crap carpet sweeper), Number 6 (tiny little fags), Slim Kings (long and very thin and extremely cool in their day), John Player Black (a bit like Death Cigarettes, or at least in myth, smoke enough in one day and the next day you couldn't speak, they were guaranteed to give you cancer, they contained more nicotine in one fag than most had in 20), Weights, Black Cat, Golden Virginia, Old Holborn, Camels, Gold Flake, Strand (good advert: *You're never alone with a Strand* with a dark shadowy figure lighting a fag with their collar up against the wind on, I think, a bridge, at night but apparently it didn't sell fags as no one wanted to be a loner), Chesterfields, Peter Stuyvesant, Rothmans, Lambert and Butler, Consulate Menthol, Lucky Strike, Capstan and, bestest of all, Woodbines, which incidentally is the real name for the climbing plant honeysuckle but its name was changed as people didn't want to plant a cigarette in their gardens. They were originally called Wild Woodbine, the fags not the plant. I think I'm on the side of the gardeners: why should they have a beautiful plant – and one with a fabulous scent – named the same as a smelly fag? It was the manufacturers who should have been made to change the name. We should have been smoking Wild Honeysuckle.

If any of this makes you think I'd smoke anything I guess you're right. I have, and would, smoke anything that was going. Remember I was an addict. If offered a fag I would have smoked it. If it was tipped I would have broken the tip off – hated tips, thought they must give you cancer as I had once seen statistics for cancer before and after World War II. The rates rocketed after the war when tips came in and untipped fags were considered uncool. I also didn't like low tar fags for the same reason. I also didn't like tobacco in American fags, preferred rolling tobacco or French. I had once heard that tobacco was cured differently for French fags and rolling tobacco – sun dried rather than artificially dried in a factory thus less cancer as it was a more natural product. Oh, how we smokers like to fool ourselves, how we like to lie to ourselves, oh how the Voice lies to us. Tools in the hands of the parasite.

Back to the dream: all these fag packets were whirling through the air and I was reaching up and taking one out of the herd, smoking a fag from it and then putting the pack back into the whirling throng. There were fag cards in there too – remember those? You got to collect cards of famous race cars, actors, film stars, Derby winners, that sort of thing. I never collected cards or coupons of Green Shield Stamps if I could help it but I did smoke Embassy for a while and gave the coupons to my brother. Yes, he once bought a crap carpet sweeper. I suppose today's crap carpet sweeper is the crap personal CD player with those tiny headphones which fall out of your ears if you move your head.

So, what do we do when we have finished our meal, had sex, had a cup of coffee and desperately want that habitual cigarette?

So, what do we do when we have finished our meal, had sex, had a cup of coffee and desperately want that habitual cigarette? Personally I don't really care what *you* do. I get up immediately and walk about, do something, wash up (after the meal not after sex), make a cup of tea, eat some fruit (apparently Vitamin C helps the body get rid of nicotine more easily). Each of these moments – sex, meals, coffee, finishing a bit of work, arriving in London on the train and not having had a fag for two and a half hours, coming out of the cinema, theatre, etc – is a punctuation point. They mark the end of something and we have a fag to celebrate that end or to mark it in some way.

If we are going to go through three months of agony giving up then it makes sense to avoid as many of these things as possible for these three months. Don't go to the cinema, stay away from London, don't eat – or rather avoid the sort of dinner parties where everyone sits around smoking and drinking wine afterwards. Hang out with non-smokers for a bit – yes, I know how boring they are but we can use them – and find something to do with your hands. Fiddle with pens, flick matches (no, probably best not to play with matches), use a Dictaphone machine and record your thoughts, emotions, panic attacks. OK, so what are we going to do about the sex one? Easy, either get up and make tea, fetch wine, wash your hands or do it again. Nothing like another bout to take your mind off the Voice.

My personal attack is to force the Voice to shut up. I know when it is going to be most active –

Oh, dear boy, how can you lie there after sex and not indulge in the warmth, the passion, the delight of that post-sexual fag? You are missing so much.

– that sort of thing. I get in first. I say: "Hey, Voice, I've just had sex, wanna berate me for not smoking? Wanna tell me about all the dead people? Wanna tell me about the children you get hooked?" It's amazing how quiet the Voice goes when it doesn't have an answer.

Oh, I have answers alright but not when you're not listening. Putting your hands over your ears and shouting "Not listening, not listening" isn't very grown up is it? All this giving up stuff is pathetic. Smoking is not that bad. Look at all the other killers – pollution, war, famine, car crashes. When it comes to Horsemen I don't even rate a small donkey.

I disagree. I think that when the Four Horsemen come you'll be up there with them. Look at how many people you must have killed. You must be up there alongside war and famine and mosquitoes.

Mosquitoes?

Yes, they have killed more human beings since the dawn of time than any thing else. But I figure you must be about equalling them by now. I've been reading about the chemicals in smoke. Here's a quick list:

2-Butane
2-Naphthylamine
3-Picoline
3-Vinylpyridine
4-Aminopiphyenyl
Acethylene
Acetone
Acetonitrile
Ammonia
Aniline
Benz(a)pyrene
Carbon Dioxide
Carbon Monoxide
Catechole
Dimethylinitrosamine
Hydrazine
Hydrogen Cyanide
Methane
Methylchloride
Methylfuran
Methylnapthalene
Methylquinolines
Napthalene
Nicotine
Nitrogen Oxides
Nitrosonornicotine
Nitrospyrrolidine
Phenol
Propane Propene
Propionaldehyde
Pyrene
Pyridine
Quinoline
Stigmasterol
Tar (this in itself has over 19 chemicals all of which are known carcinogens)
Toluene

Isn't that lot fun? Don't you just love carbon monoxide and cyanide? I mean even I know they're poisons. Even a dumbo like me knows you don't breathe that stuff in. So what the hell have I been breathing in all these years?

The more I research this stuff the less I like smoking. Now, don't get me wrong. I'm not turning all anti-smoking on you but my eyes are being opened a little. I am beginning to question. I am beginning to dislike the manufacturers more and more. I find it a bit offensive that my habit, my addiction might just have been engineered deliberately to line their pockets. I mean, that's a bit nasty, don't you think? But then again they too are in the grip of the parasite.

I've also been reading about the by-products of smoking – apart from the pleasure of course:

For smokers, the specific health risks of tobacco use include:

- Nicotine addiction
- Decreased senses of taste and smell
- Increased foetal death and diseases for women
- Lung disease including emphysema, chronic bronchitis, lung cancer
- Coronary artery disease – angina, heart attacks
- Atherosclerotic and peripheral vascular disease – aneurysms, hypertension, blood clots, strokes
- Oral/tooth/gum diseases – including oral cancer

For non-smokers exposed regularly to second hand smoke, the specific health risks include:

- Increased risk of lung cancer over those not exposed to smoke – looks like the passive smoking brigade might actually have something after all
- In children there is an increased incidence of respiratory infections (such as bronchitis and pneumonia), asthma, and declining lung function as the lungs mature
- Non-smokers can experience (upon exposure to smoke) acute, sudden, and occasionally severe, reactions including eye, nose, throat, and lower respiratory tract symptoms

The interesting thing is the number of times people have tried to give up. We all try loads of times and each time we 'fail' we regard ourselves as pathetic, failures, no will power. Each time lessens our self-esteem which can lead us to smoke more. It's a sort of vicious downward spiral. But, and here is hope: we have to try many times to eventually be successful. If we don't go through this process of trying, failing, trying, failing, trying, succeeding we won't ever give up. It's a bit like selling. You have to make 20 phone calls to get that one sale. You have to give up 20 times to make that one successful attempt. Each time you give up and fail put it down to experience – ah, I've not failed, just found another method that doesn't work for me.

You may have to give up 20 times to make that one successful attempt

And look at the benefits of not smoking:

- *Within 20 minutes* of giving up your blood pressure and pulse rate return to normal and the body temperature of your extremities – hands and feet – increase to normal
- *Within 8 hours* of not smoking the carbon monoxide levels in your blood drop and normal oxygen levels rise
- *24 hours:* The risk of heart attack decreases
- *48 hours:* Regeneration of nerve endings (and you didn't even know they'd been shot away did you?) and return to normal of sense of smell and taste
- *Fortnight to 3 months:* Circulation improves and walking becomes easier with lung function increasing and improving by up to 30%
- *1 to 9 months:* Overall energy increase, coughing and nasal congestion, fatigue, shortness of breath, cilia return to normal (fine hairs lining lower respiratory tract which handle mucus and clean the tract), reduced respiratory infections
- *1 year:* Coronary heart disease reduced by half
- *5 years:* Lung cancer rates halved as is cancer of the mouth
- *10 years:* Mouth cancer rates have dropped by over half and lung cancer rates to those of non smokers, pre-cancerous cells being replaced with normal healthy cell growth, risk of stroke lowered – almost down to that of non-smokers. Cancer of bladder and kidney and pancreas decreases
- *15 years:* risk of heart attack same as that of someone who never smoked

Powerful stuff. I've always run a mile from this sort of thing when I was smoking. If it makes you feel queasy please feel free to skip any of it especially if you are smoking at the moment and well in the grip of the Voice. It'll be saying:

Oh, dear boy, don't bother reading this stuff. You won't get cancer. I'll protect you. Smoking makes you relax so you won't get bowel cancer. Stress related disorders are much more prevalent. Smoking chills you. Don't read this propaganda.

I think if you do want to stop you need some form of motivation. For me this has been realising that tobacco is a parasite (where is that Nobel prize?). You also need confidence – it is bearable, you can do it, you are not alone, this thing can be defeated, you can win – and commitment. There's not a lot of point in just talking about giving up. You either pack it in or you don't. Cutting down is a waste of space.

If you do want to stop you need confidence

Look, I love smoking. I think smoking is cool. But I ain't gonna do it no more. Reason? I don't like being in the grip of a parasite. I don't like being a host. You may think this crazy seeing as how I was quite happy to be addicted for 35 years give or take a decade. And I was. Quite, quite happy to be addicted. But not happy to be a host. Addiction – and they say tobacco is more addictive than heroin – is a random, chance thing, a sort of by-product of smoking. But parasitic hosting is deliberate. I've been targeted and I don't like it. I'm being used. I don't mind using tobacco but I don't like tobacco using me.

It's a meeting of two individuals, two equals. There is no using of anyone by anything. We both need each other, my dear boy. Can't you see that?

I see parasitic hosting for what it is. I am not prepared to be a host. It is as simple as that. If this is what it takes to get me through, to give up, to pack it in, then that is what I'm going to do, going to think about, going to focus on.

That and reducing my arthritis. Since stopping there has been a quite marked reduction in swelling of ankles and knees. This may be down to Christian whom I have been back to see twice. He says my energy is getting more normal – i.e. in my body where it is supposed to be apparently. Or it may be down to not smoking. According to research smoking can trigger a genetic reaction that leads to a more severe form of rheumatoid arthritis. Look I always said I would give up smoking if it affected my health. What I meant was if I got breathless or wheezy – Roni does say I was getting pretty wheezy at night when I was asleep which has cleared up since I gave up – or coughed up blood, that sort of thing. I didn't mean arthritis but seeing as how it has struck me down and seeing as how it is clearing up now I have stopped smoking, I guess smoking was affecting my health in subtle ways I hadn't bargained for.

Smoking may also trigger rheumatism as well as giving arthritis sufferers a more severe version of the disease. I was getting it pretty painfully. Apparently smoking increases the production of the rheumatoid factor which is the substance in the blood they check for to see if you've got rheumatoid arthritis. Smokers get more joint damage, increased chances of getting diabetes, most of the cancers (70% of all people who die from some form of cancer are smokers – bugger), cataracts, long term hearing loss (no, I have no idea why smokers go deaf more often than non-smokers, probably having to block your ears to all those facts about smoking killing you).

While researching this I did discover that coffee can also trigger this severe form of rheumatoid arthritis so I've switched to decaffeinated for a while to see if this makes any difference. Trouble is I am trying so many things at once I have no idea what is working and what isn't. I don't care. I'm not smoking and the arthritis is clearing up. I think I'm beginning to feel better about this. I don't want to go on too much about the death stuff and the addiction stuff and the chemicals et al but it is interesting what rubbish we are taking into our bodies when we smoke. God, I sound like a non-smoker and that was something I promised I would never do. There is nothing worse than a born again evangelising non-smoker who tut tuts every time some one lights up a fag.

God, I sound like a non-smoker and that was something I promised I would never do. There is nothing worse than a born again evangelising non-smoker who tut tuts every time some one lights up a fag

I've just found another of those deduct x amount of time per fag smoked statistics. This one says it is 3 hours 40 minutes per pack of 20. That's the same as the 11 minutes a fag calculation, but another way of looking at how much time you cost yourself for every day you smoke. Suppose I was destined to live to 95, smoking means I'm going to croak at 89. Thank god it's off the end of my life and not in the middle, or even the beginning. Roni has a story about someone signing a pact with the devil for limitless fun, money etc in exchange for a mere five years off their life. Seems like a bargain at the time but the devil takes those five years from the beginning of the chap's life. Bugger. That means no language development, no walking, no dressing yourself, no emotional response, no nothing basically. Tricky devil the devil. Bit like the Voice. Strangely hypnotic. Strangely seductive and oily. Best avoided at all costs.

Hey, don't equate me with the devil. I'm your friend. I don't want to corrupt you, only to please you, to serve you, to make you happy. I don't want your soul. I don't do pacts or bargains or promises. Look, I know the evidence is stacking up against me but I can assure you the charges are entirely false. It's all propaganda. It's all lies. This stuff about death and cancer is put about by the non-smoking brigade, the killjoys, the sad beggars who can't stand to see anyone enjoying themselves. Don't listen. Shut up your ears and listen to me.

Don't go onto the Internet and look up this stuff. It will only upset you. Better to sit back and have a fag and let it all wash over you. Are you happier now? No. Are you more relaxed? No. Are you sleeping better at night? No. Are you eating better? No. Are you less twitchy, less nervy, less jumpy? No. Can you honestly say not smoking is satisfying you? No. Can you honestly, hand on heart hope to die in a cellar full of rats, say that not smoking is where you really, really want to be?

Yes. No. Perhaps. Maybe. I don't know.

And maybe it's time I fought back a bit. Pin your ears back laddie while I tell you a few home truths about this disgusting habit – your words, not mine – that you have packed in. Smoking isn't all bad you know. Smoking protects you from the risk of developing Parkinson's disease – University of Birmingham Neurology department and backed up by the Parkinson's Disease Society. Smokers are at less risk of contracting Alzheimer's – Duke University Medical Center in North Carolina – and those with the disease can enjoy remission if they begin smoking. How's that for starters, sonny?

Stalwart Insurance is offering special rates to smokers paying up to 3% more than standard annuities for non-smokers. It's bad enough you guys get taxed so much but now someone is recognising that smokers don't die as early as the scaremongers say.

And smokers who pop out for a fag during office hours in non-smoking offices were found to be enjoying life more, bonding better, exchanging information more freely and generally breaking down hierarchical barriers – FT. Smokers make better managers and nicer people. Check out 'Get More From Your Work – And More Fun' by Neasa MacErlean.

'Nature' magazine reports that the number of accidents and injuries in the workplace soar every time there is a National No Smokes day. Most of these accidents can be put down to a loss of concentration. Nicotine does aid that if nothing else. And that has been scientifically proved at McLean Hospital in Belmont, Massachusetts using brain scans on smokers and non-smokers. Smokers had more brain activity in the concentration areas. So there, ya boo sucks.

Work done at Virginia University showed nicotine could act as an analgesic. And 'New Scientist' magazine has reported that in a small number of cases cigarette smoking may prevent breast cancer. The Women's College of Toronto found that for 1 in 250 women who carry mutated genes which give them an 80% probability of developing breast cancer, smoking 20 fags a day for four years reduces the chance of developing the disease by 53%.

On the 9th of April 1999 Henry Doubleday celebrated his 100th birthday. His secret of long life? He's smoked continuously since he was six years old. Put that in your pipe and smoke it.

Stanford University has reported that small doses of nicotine appear to promote new blood vessel growth and may help heart attack sufferers.

Nicotine may provide the breakthrough in the search for a vaccine against the HIV virus. Researchers at CropTech are working on genetically altering tobacco leaf to provide a protein found in two strains of HIV in the hope of providing a vaccine.

So you are not the only one who can quote statistics to make their case. You're not the only one who can look things up on the Internet. You're not the only one who can draw inferences, make assumptions, derive quantum leaps from tiny research trials. You're not alone, kiddo. But the biggest thing about smoking isn't quantity of life. Sure you might live another three years, or five, or 10. But what sort of a life is it when you can't sit back after a good meal and light an expensive cigar? What sort of life do you really look forward to when you can't have a fag after sex or with a cup of coffee? What sort of life is it where the killjoys, the scaremongers, the non-smokers, the puritans have won the day? What sort of world is it when even French cafés are banning smoking?

You can't smoke on trains, at the cinema, at the office, near children. Will you all lie down and take it when smoking is banned in the park, while boating, on beaches, even in the Antarctic? When the killjoys roll over you, will you all just give in and shut up and capitulate? Because if you do then this life will have no quality, only quantity. It won't be a life worth living. It will be grey and drear and sad. You will be dull and boring and pathetic.

What happened to the rock and roll, the rebellion, the life to be lived against quiet desperation revolution? What has happened to you? You've gone soft my lad, soft. You might as well hang up the leather jacket and get the slippers out, book a caravan holiday, sell the open top sports car, take the pledge, and then quietly open your veins and slip into oblivion. You may not be dead but you might as well be. Goodbye happiness. Farewell wild times. So long deep smug satisfaction, the sort where you could fold your hands across your belly and relax back into your chair with a fresh roll-up, a good story, a glass of red wine and a collection of like minded souls around you.

I shan't smoke again even if it does mean getting a caravan

Whew. The Voice has made a strong case. So strong I'm severely tempted to have a fag. It's only the sense of the dancing skull hidden behind the sweet words that stops me. Yes, I've gone soft. That hurt. Yes, the leather jacket might as well be hung up. That hurt too. But

I look forward to seeing my kids get married, have children, start successful careers. I might not be around for ever for them but I would like to see them well on their way. Tobacco claimed Pop, the man I loved. I shan't smoke again even if it does mean getting a caravan.

"The cigarette should be conceived not as a product but as a package. The product is nicotine....Think of the cigarette pack as a storage container for a day's supply of nicotine....Think of a cigarette as a dispenser for a dose unit of nicotine. Think of a puff of smoke as the vehicle of nicotine....Smoke is beyond question the most optimised vehicle of nicotine and the cigarette the most optimised dispenser of smoke."

Philip Morris, 1972

Chapter 6

Month 3

"Now the only thing I miss about sex is the cigarette afterward. Next to the first one in the morning, it's the best one of all. It tasted so good that even if I had been frigid I would have pretended otherwise just to be able to smoke it."

Florence King

I think it's getting easier. I am sleeping better. I've cut down on the brandy, a lot. I'm feeling happier and working again. Yes, it's been a long slog. I feel bruised and battered. I feel as if I've gone through a major struggle and am just beginning to come out of it. It's too early to be able to say I've done it and people congratulating me still makes me feel incredibly odd, as if I haven't done anything to deserve praise. I should have deserved praise if I had never taken it up in the first place. I've been weak for 40 years and now I've been strong for less than three months people are saying well done and that sort of stuff. It doesn't seem well balanced somehow.

I still smell of soap and I still want to eat a lot. I have avoided putting on weight but I'm not sure how. I have gorged, at times, on chocolate and sweets. I have eaten a lot of fruit and nibbled a lot of nuts. I have used whatever resources were available to get me through. I've drunk a lot of water as it seems to alleviate the withdrawal pangs.

I dream of smoking a lot and am always relieved to wake up and find I haven't really given in

My lungs still seem tight. I still get panicky feelings if anyone smokes near me. I have held a cigarette and not felt any compulsion to light one. I have sat next to smokers smoking at parties and not been tempted. I dream of smoking a lot and am always relieved to wake up and find I haven't really given in. I don't feel any healthier particularly but these things are so hard to judge. My arthritis is better. I'm not dancing or running yet but that would be undignified for a man of my standing anyway.

Getting smug?

No. Just jotting down for the people exactly what is going on for me. Throughout this book I have tried to be honest. To say it's hard. I haven't tried to paint a picture of giving up as a doddle or easy or fun. It ain't. It's hard. I'm not crowing. I'm not smug. I'm not even quietly confident I won't return to the fold – and that is how I still see it. I feel alone and an outsider. I have shunned my friends and my principles and my big robust lifestyle. I feel thin and pale and sad. I am not smoking but not yet a non-smoker.

I haven't turned judgmental which is a blessed relief. People still smoke in my house and that is OK. I can still smell a smoker in the street and find myself recoiling in horror – it's a bad smell. I still like the smell of roll-ups around me though. I still latch on to the sight of a fag in films or on the telly (increasingly rare) and have been known to tune in secretly just to see Dot Cotton enjoying a fag.

I still sit back and pat my pockets for the disappeared kit of baccy, papers and lighter whenever I have finished anything. I have to get up immediately and walk about, look out of the window, make some tea, fiddle with something, wind a clock, scratch my bum, let the dogs out, rearrange objects on my desk, breath deeply and go and clean my teeth yet again to try and get rid of the disgusting taste which I only realise after I have cleaned them is the taste of clean teeth. Quite disgusting. Where has my tongue fur gone? Why does my mouth always taste of tea or peppermint toothpaste? – but God, never peppermint tea, I'd slit my wrists if I were reduced to drinking herbal teas. Why do my hands smell of soap? Why are there no nicotine stains on my fingers anymore? Why is my little pumice stone now redundant? It's all a bit like grieving after someone close has died. You still look for them in all the old familiar places, but they aren't there any more.

I had to go to London again the other day for work and opened my laptop on the train. I haven't used it in quite a while and lots of little bits of tobacco fell out. I was quite nostalgic but also revolted. Did everything in my life used to be covered in little bits of tobacco? Roni opened a book the other day that she knew I had been the last person to look at, and a little puff of ash fell out. How sad.

I have binged on chocolate – have I said this already? I figure chocolate isn't addictive. I'm not up to 20 bars a day yet. I can always lose weight after I've got this bugger beat. Is it better to be fat or to smoke? Answers please, I'm serious.

It's a bit like grieving after someone close has died. You still look for them in all the old familiar places, but they aren't there any more

I'm still not sure who I am not smoking. I used to be roll-up Rich, rolly Rich, the roll-up Craze, the latest smoking Craze. Now who am I? I don't know yet. I'm trying to be as big and as robust as before but I do feel tamed, smaller, greyer, sadder, more normal, less rebellious. The Voice was quite right even if its motives were quite wrong.

I have developed a really itchy scalp. I think I spend a lot of time scratching my head instead of smoking. I have worn little scabby bits but at least they're not cancerous, or at least I hope they're not.

I think one of the things that is keeping me from smoking is I couldn't bear the smug Voice saying: I told you so, if I ever took it up again.

I wouldn't. I would congratulate you on your serious grown up decision to do something courageous, something rebellious, to fly in the face of convention, to be your own man, to be slick and suave and sophisticated. I would buy you a drink, slap you on the back, shake your hand and be your buddy. I would think you had made a smart decision. There would be no smugness. There would be no sense of failure. You would be the prodigal son not the object of pity. I would be warm and affectionate. I would love you just as much as I do now. You may have turned your back on me after we've been together for so long but I would forgive you instantly. I wouldn't hold a grudge. I would be your buddy again, old buddy, dear boy.

Yuck. Doesn't it ever stop? How long do I have to put up with this crap? I wish there were other words for 'quitting', 'non-smoker', 'giving up', 'packing it in', 'passive smoking'. These are all victim words, weasel words. I want words of power. I want proactive words. I want words that make me feel good, make me feel like a doer not a be-done-to. Quitting smoking isn't easy and we who manage it shouldn't be made to feel we are giving up but rather taking up something else. God, I'd hate it but we ought to say we are choosing health rather than giving up smoking – taking up health perhaps? I've no idea what these words should be, I just don't like the ones we've got.

I was looking at a questionnaire completed on National No Smoking Day in 1999 (MORI poll) and it's quite interesting. Apparently if you want to avoid smokers then don't hang out in pubs because this is where 83% of people say they encounter smoke and if they are trying to give it up find this the worse place to be. Cafés and restaurants came second with some 61% of people saying they encountered smoke there. Third was the homes of friends at 45%. So you know where to avoid if you want to get over that three month hump. But smokers, when asked, said that they wanted to see smoking banned in restaurants (25%) and pubs (22%) but only 7% thought it would be a good idea to have it banned in the homes of friends. Shows how considerate smokers are.

It's interesting that the native American peoples (Red Indians when I was a kid) smoked *nicotiana rustica* which gives you such a head rush that it becomes a hallucinogen but the early Europeans didn't like that idea and spread the use of *nicotiana tabacum* which is a less potent tropical strain of the plant. Bugger, we didn't even get the good stuff. We gave them syphilis, drunkenness and the American way of life and they gave us cheap tobacco. It was the same in South America. We, the Europeans, gave them a whole bunch of crap including the Conquistadors and all they gave us was their gold – oh yes, and cocaine.

I got an email from BJ Cunningham the other day saying how he had given up smoking. Well, how he'd given it up until he bumped into his friend Spike. Spike has a great line about smoking being a psychological addiction and you should be the master of it and not the other way round. If you're really in control you can have a fag after you've given up and not start smoking again. BJ thought this a brilliant philosophy and had to buy a pack to try it out. He's hooked again. I think Spike is as big an addict as the rest of us, he's just not admitting it. He says he can give up any time he wants to. Yeah, right. Didn't we all say that once?

I think he is right.

You can shut up straight away.

I still think the secret is *wanting* to want to give up. It is the first step. It is the first shot in the war which must be waged in the mind. Before I gave up this time I was conscious of wanting to want to give up. I had been practising not smoking for a couple of months before I took the plunge. This might have been nothing more than catching myself not smoking and noticing and saying: "See, Rich, you're not smoking at this very minute and you're doing fine". I might immediately panic and choose to have a fag but quite often I didn't.

I just carried on not smoking until the proper time to have a fag. But for those few moments I was consciously not smoking and surviving, doing fine. It made me realise that it was possible to go without a fag.

I was not smoking for 22 and 1/2 hours a day

I was also adding up how long I was smoking a day. I reckoned that each fag lasted five minutes and I smoked, on average, 20 a day. Therefore 5 x 20 = 100 minutes = $1^1/_2$ of an hour a day. Therefore this means I was not smoking for $22^1/_2$ hours a day.

Now what was I doing for over 22 hours? Was I in a cold sweat? No. Was I shaking, twitchy, unable to work, to sleep, to eat properly? No. Was I dreaming of fags? No. Were cigarettes occupying every waking thought? No. I then rationalised that smoking actually took up a very little of my life and anything that was that insignificant could be got rid of. Yes, I know all about the addiction etc but in my mind I had already disposed of this tiny threat to my sanity. It doesn't matter if I was wrong in my reasoning or mad or stupid or anything – I had already begun the battle to beat the monster in my mind. If you don't do that you ain't going to win.

I got asked the other day – by a non-smoker of course – if the warnings on fag packs had ever had any effect. Of course not. WARNING: Cigarettes cause death. Yeah, right. But which one? Which is the fag which actually gives you cancer? Identify that one and don't smoke it and you're safe. Each fag, in isolation, isn't a danger. They each drip their tiny bit of poison but individually they don't hurt you. OK, since taking up smoking I might well have smoked around 300,000 fags. God, that frightened even me when I worked it out: 40 years x 365 days x 20 fags.

Incidentally, I found a good website – silkquit.org – they allow you to download a quit meter. This keeps score – so many days without a fag, so many fags not smoked, so much money saved, so many minutes added back onto your life. Brilliant. Apparently it does stop some people taking up smoking again as they don't want to reset the meter. I set the meter running when I stopped and it has already been quite an eye opener. It sits on my computer desktop and clicks away the seconds and the fags not smoked so that it is constantly updated. I don't think I would like to reset it either.

Anyway, back to the ineffectualness of health warnings. Assume that you only get cancer once you've smoked more than a certain number or for more than a certain number of years and you begin to get inside the mind of the smoker – this won't hurt me as I intend giving up before I reach that certain number.

Of course we don't. Of course we don't look at how many, how much we really smoke because all we do is concentrate on that one tiny fag that we are smoking at the time. Smoking keeps you very present, in the here and now so you don't think about the future. Smoking is a form of meditation, no, it really is. It keeps you mindful, present, concentrated. Each inhale and exhale is an affirmation of life and the rhythm of the cosmos. Sorry, getting a bit wibbly. I'll shut up.

Who cares that you might die one day in the future because when you are young there is so much future to come. At my age I feel that there might just be more behind me than in front and it gets very scary. I have no idea what happens to us when we do die but I don't want to rush headlong into it before I'm ready.

And when will you be ready? And will you seriously face such a momentous act without a fag to steady your nerves? Oh, I don't think so.

Millions and millions of people faced death before tobacco was introduced into the Western world and did so without a fag.

Yes, but I bet they all felt they were missing something and just didn't know what. I am the best invention mankind has ever made. I am a gift from the gods. I am the Emperor of Dreams. I am your help and your delight.

And my early death and my hacking cough and my children's temptation. You are seducer and damnation. You would hurry me to my death. I think I'll hang back a bit even if it does mean not smoking.

I was always there for you in times of peril.

Yes, you were and I was grateful. Now I am going to try doing it alone, without help, no props.

Just you hope and pray nothing really bad happens to you soon or you're going to regret that decision.

Don't threaten me.

The non-smoker who asked me if the death threats on the packs used to have any influence on me has never smoked, ever. Roy says that not one cigarette has ever touched his lips. He has never taken one single drag on a fag, ever. I found this almost impossible to believe. I remember all those sessions when I was a kid when we gathered at the back of the scout hut, bike sheds, naval cadet hut, in the bogs, wherever, for a shared fag – all berating the obnoxious kid who slobbered on the end of the fag and made it all wet or the bully who took more than his share or the puffer who didn't inhale properly. All in all we were a pretty pathetic bunch. *My* role? Oh, I was the kid who always had the fags. But poor Roy has never participated in such elemental bonding, has never enjoyed such forbidden pleasures. I asked him why and he said:

- Smoking made your breath smell
- It was addictive and he had never gone for that
- It was expensive
- It adversely affects your lungs
- He couldn't see what you got out of it – missed the pleasure principle altogether

But Roy does go to the pub for lunch everyday. He has a pint or two and returns to work. Now I don't drink beer. I may have the occasional lager but as for drinking bitter I have never indulged. The reasons?

– It makes your breath smell
– Beer is addictive
– It is expensive
– It adversely affects your liver
– I can't see what people get out of it

Basically we have the same objections to each other's habit – smelly, expensive, unhealthy, not personally attractive. But it is odd that Roy berates me for having been a smoker whereas I'm quite happy for him to be a drinker. It ain't hurting me so why should I criticise him? My smoke has never hurt him as I've never smoked around him. So what's his problem? Why can't we smokers be left to enjoy our habit without people censuring us? We don't tell others how to carry on, so what gives non-smokers the right to interfere, to tell us how to behave? And now I've become a not smoking sort of person I shall not criticise others for doing it.

Just because I have seen the truth behind the parasite doesn't mean I shall embark on a crusade. No way, not ever. I used to know a chap who, once he had given up, would snatch the cigarettes out of people's mouths in the street. Well, he did this until he got a slap. That put a stop to his japes.

Now I've become a not smoking sort of person I shall not criticise others for doing it

When things go wrong – you buy a crap product from Comet and they won't take it back (I'm banned from my local Comet store for losing my rag when they wouldn't replace a video player I had bought), the train is late and you miss a vital appointment, the washing machine breaks down and spews suds all over the floor, the car breaks down miles from anywhere and there is no service on your mobile – I have this overwhelming urge to smoke and then shout "Now look what you made me do, it's all your fault."

Sounds reasonable to me.

Shut up.

I was in a garage the other day waiting to pay for my petrol when the chap in front of me asked for some Golden Virginia. I stood trans-fixed. This was me in a past life. He was asked for the money – about £2.34 or something like that – and immediately started complaining. "Is that what it is these days?" I realised I was standing behind a not smoker who was about to go back to the monster. This was a man listening to the Voice. What could I do? I wanted to snatch the pack of tobacco from his hand and hurl it to the floor. But I remembered my friend's punch in the mouth and controlled myself.

Can you still get those crap rolling machines? I have no idea. I remember them though. One of my brothers had one and I thought it so uncool, so girlie, so amateurish that I would only use it when no one was looking. It was the same brother who taught me how to roll a proper fag. It was in the scout hut around 1965. We sat together waiting for some other scouts to return with the jumble sale cart – they went out collecting – and were having a crafty smoke. I rolled a fag and he said it was crap and then proceeded to show me how to do it properly. I thought I was doing OK but there was a certain difference; what he showed me did make the fag look better, more grown up, cooler.

He is a brother who has survived – at the time of writing – but still smokes on and off. My oldest brother didn't make it. He died two years ago. Not through smoking but through drinking. He had a long term problem controlling his drinking and finally fell off some concrete steps while drunk and died eventually of massive head injuries. I hope my tone is not judgmental as I wouldn't like you to think I looked down on his drinking. He smoked but it was the alcohol that was his own private demon, his downfall if you'll excuse the most dreadful pun I have ever made in my life.

I think one of the reasons I smoked was because he smoked. We used to holiday in St Ives and we stayed in B&Bs. The eldest was put in the same room as the youngest – him with me – to keep us both out of trouble. I would behave being with a biggie and he couldn't bring girls back as a littlie was there. You have to admire my mother's clever reasoning. It worked to a certain extent but I did know him on the odd occasion slip out in the early hours. I was supposed to be asleep and he was supposed to be looking after me. Neither of us said anything. It was an arrangement which we both enjoyed. I felt very grown up being left (I must have been about eight) and he got a shag (he must have been about 18). He would lie in bed smoking and I would watch that little red ember as we talked and I thought it the most romantic, evocative thing I had ever seen.

Back to the crap rolling machines. You could buy filters to put in them which had the consistency of shredded stiffened cotton wool – nowadays I think it's the same stuff they use to make fleeces – and they collected all the nicotine in a little slimy pool of brown at the end of the roll up. They really were revolting. I went through a phase of smoking liquorice papers – they tasted of shit rather than liquorice and were the same colour – because I thought they looked cool and arty. Oh, the stuff I have smoked because I thought it looked cool and arty.

I took up smoking dope because it was cool and arty. At the age of 16 I was smoking dope. My mother went out one evening and I had a spliff – we called them joints in those long ago days – but on her return she asked what the funny smell was. I quickly said I had been smoking herbal cigarettes but she said that was funny because it smelt just like marijuana and then walked out of the room. "Hey, come back little old lady. What do you mean?" She said "Oh, you young kids think you've invented everything. We smoked them in the jazz clubs during the war; we called them reefers. Got any left?" Yep, I shared a spliff/joint/reefer with my mother at that tender age.

Oh, the stuff I have smoked because I thought it looked cool and arty. I took up smoking dope because it was cool and arty

Now, I'm not advocating drug use/abuse in any form. I don't do drugs, but young people will always experiment especially if they think they look cool and arty – or is it called wicked these days? – and who am I to judge when I've done it?

I think my mother was secretly pleased with herself being so liberated and wacky. Did she approve of drugs? No, most definitely not but she saw smoking a little dope as part of social life like a gin and tonic. She approved of smoking and I remember her giving me two bob (about 10p) for a packet of fags when I was 14 and we had fallen out. And when my eldest brother was in hospital – after another drunken fall when he split his nose open – and my mother and I went to see him and I was quite shocked at the state he was in she gave me a fag on the bus on the way home to calm my nerves. I was 13 or so.

She did give it up herself for a few years after she had been wheeled into hospital with acute appendicitis. She came round from the operation and simply didn't smoke. This is someone going from 80 a day to none at all literally overnight. No withdrawal, no side effects, nothing at all. Weird or what? I think she only took it up again because she wanted to look cool and arty in her old age.

The funny thing was that when she returned to it she switched from Players full strength untipped to those dreadful tipped Peter Stuyvesant. I couldn't understand that one. Players were wonderful, tasty, strong, meaty, somehow a professional smoke. Stuyvesant were weak and insipid, thin and girlie. They also seemed unhealthy to me, an indoor smoke rather that a healthy outdoor rugged sailor's fag like Players were. She didn't smoke as many but kept up the habit right to the end – or almost to the very end.

I did make the mistake of offering her a fag when she had just been diagnosed with lung cancer and given two weeks to live. She said to me quite calmly, "Don't be so bloody silly" and then told me why. I was a little taken aback I can tell you. I guess she realised that smoking wasn't cool or arty a bit too late and I hope to avoid that one myself. She nearly smoked to the very end but gave it up for her last two weeks. She seemed happy to go and said she was tired. Obviously the morphine helped her through it. This was 10 years ago and I don't think she would have liked to have got older and more crippled with arthritis and helpless. She was a difficult, game old bird who loved life and wouldn't have wanted to end up in a home. She lived big if you know what I mean. I remember sharing that spliff with her and I remember her as active and energetic and robust. I'm glad I never got to see her decrepit and old and helpless either.

Whoa! It's all getting a bit morbid here and I was telling you what Month 3 has been like.

I'll tell you what it has been like for him. He has craved the delicious taste of my most noble self every day. He has been edgy and lacking in concen-tra-tion. He doesn't look cool or arty any more. He is a sad pale reflection of himself. He has no identity, no character, no personality. He has become a non-smoker and he is beginning to be proud of that. He is a sad wretch. He sits in the non-smoking section of restaurants trying so damn hard not to look smug. I won't sit with him any more. He smells of soap.

Yep, it's still been tough but I dare say it's getting easier. Yes, I still dream of smoking. I still crave it. My lungs still feel tight but I do believe things are getting better. I have gone the odd whole day with barely a thought about it. I have managed to sit next to a smoker and not try to suck their smoke into my lungs. I have even given away the last pack of tobacco I had when I stopped. My son Rufus came down with his girlfriend and they ran out of tobacco late one night. I nobly gave them my pack which I had framed along with the last papers and the last lighter. It had no hold over me and I didn't even need it as a memento.

I have stopped. I'm not out of the woods yet but I can begin to see daylight. I will feel free after a year of this but realise I could go back to it at the drop of a hat or any major crisis in my life. Luckily the gods are being good to me at the moment and things aren't going wrong too often or too seriously.

My lungs still feel tight but I do believe things are getting better

A series of tough anti-cigarette adverts has been launched in the UK with the message that smoking is bad for your sex life because it makes men impotent and women ugly – God that it would make ugly men impotent. The campaign is designed to target young people's fears about sexual attractiveness; an area the government says is more effective than highlighting their general health concerns.

One ad targets women by saying cigarettes lead to premature skin ageing, minging teeth and warns that smoking causes "cat's bum mouth". Another of the adverts aims to frighten men by using a burning cigarette end between fingers to look like legs to look like a penis with the punchline "Does smoking make you hard? Not if it means you can't get it up". The government says smoking increases the risk of erectile dysfunction by around half for men in their 30s and 40s. It also claims that up to 120,000 British men within this age group were impotent as a result of smoking.

Simon Clark, director of pro-smoking group Forest says: "To try and suggest that smoking is a major cause of impotence is a scare tactic, it shows how desperate the anti-smoking campaign is. It is almost an attempt to ostracise smokers from normal society."

There was a wonderful programme on the telly the other evening all about the trade in fake fags. I had never heard of this. Apparently in China and lots of eastern European countries they make fake fags. They even make fake packets for them to go in so you can buy imitation Bensons or whatever your fancy is. The tobacco is adulterated with sawdust and other stuff but they are cheap. The programme was saying this is a really bad thing as they are unhealthy.

Oh really? I never realised fags were unhealthy! Apparently the fake ones have a much higher nicotine content. Brilliant. This is what we smokers want. *And*, and this was the biggie, the bastards were even duplicating the UK DUTY PAID printing on the packet thus depriving the Customs and Excise of their cut. But these people are crooks. The programme seemed to be saying that this printing the duty thing was really bad, immoral, naughty, against the law. Yes, faking fags is against the law. Criminals break the law, that's what they do, that's their bag, that's how they make their living. To lambast them for fake printing seemed to be the least of their misdemeanours.

I like the idea of fake fags – do you get fake illnesses? – and apparently they are sold on street corners by shifty looking individuals with their collar up and a carrier bag brimming with them. They are so good you can't tell the difference between them and smuggled ones. I always bought smuggled tobacco when I could get it as it was so much cheaper. Now I realise I might have been smoking fake tobacco. Sometimes the tobacco did seem a bit stringy with stalks in it which I assumed had failed to be spotted by Golden Virginia's quality control. I used to moan about how lumpy the tobacco was these days never dreaming I was smoking something grown in China. God, it could have been harmful. Think of the damage I could have been doing to my lungs.

Now I want to talk to you directly. I said in the introduction that this wasn't a book about you. It was/is a book about me. It is a book about me not smoking and that I didn't give a toss whether you give up or not, or have already given up and are reading this to pat yourself on the back, or are a committed smoker who has no intention of giving up and just bought it so you could laugh at me as I struggle through this and suffer pain and indignity and humiliation on your behalf… but this isn't strictly true. I do care that you give up – or want to want to give up. You see if you read this and do give up you'll tell your friends and they'll read it – having bought their own copy

I trust (don't share yours, you may need it again one day). They will also give up and the message will get passed on. I know what you're thinking: I promised not to go on a crusade. Dear friend, I have no intention of doing any such thing. I want this message to spread not because I want a world full of non-smokers but because more and more people will buy this book and thus make me a great deal of money. See, I told you it was all about me.

"The first thing you have to understand is that the filter is not a health device. The filter is a marketing device."

Fritz Gahagan, former Market Research Executive

Chapter 7

Over 100 Days

"I used to smoke two packs a day and I just hate being a non-smoker.... but I will never consider myself a non-smoker because I always find smokers the most interesting people at the table."

Michelle Pfeiffer

I can't quite believe that I am still not smoking. It feels really weird. I am a smoker. I live and eat and breathe smoking. But I am not doing it. Will I go back to smoking? I don't know. I feel I'm watching life through glass at the moment, nothing is quite real so I am protected from the reality of not smoking. What does the Voice say? It says:

Oh, yes, you will smoke again. There is no doubt about that. I am your Dark Lord and you will obey. It is only a question of time. I will catch you off guard one lonely cold winter's evening and you will come back to me. You will return to the fold and I will be triumphant.

It does feel a bit like that. I am constantly on my guard but can I maintain this vigil? Can I be this strong? I don't know. The forbidden nature, now that everyone knows I am not smoking, is so strong.

Mind you, keeping this diary has helped. I would urge anyone to do the same. It has been fascinating listening to the Voice, hearing the lies, the drivel it spouts. It has been an interesting exercise having to write down each day how I feel, what I've been going through, what physical changes have taken place. I do miss the fags, there is no doubt about that. There are no endings at the moment; it is all flow and no punctuation points. The Voice says that is unnatural and is something I really should avoid. If only I could just have the one I would be fine, but I know where that one would lead… and then I would be back to doing it every day, all the time, addicted again.

Keeping this diary has helped. I would urge anyone to do the same

And who is to say I am not still addicted? I read the other day that it only takes 48 hours for the nicotine craving to wear off. And here I am after over 100 days and still the craving is a strong as ever. It doesn't feel like 100 days but like only a few minutes since my last cigarette. My lungs are tight and my breathing shallow and fast. I crave like I've always craved.

Will I go back to it? I don't know. I really don't know.

I do. You will.

Bugger off.

"The claim that cigarette smoking causes physical dependence is simply an unproven attempt to find some way to differentiate smoking from other behaviours. The claims that smokers are 'addicts' defy common sense and contradict the fact that people quit smoking every day."

Tobacco Institute, 1988

Chapter 8

Four years on

"The cigarette does the smoking – you're just the sucker."

Anon

As I sit down to write this after at just about four fagless years, my one overwhelming thought is 'God, I could do with a ciggie'. But hold on a moment. Is it? Is it really? I'm not so sure any more.

I do still crave. I do still suddenly sit bolt upright in bed in the middle of the night desperately ashamed of myself for being a non smoker. See, I even think of myself now as a non smoker. Not an ex-smoker or a not smoker but a non smoker. See how low I have fallen? But it feels OK strangely. I don't broadcast the fact – it would be bad for my image – but secretly I'm pleased, secretly I gloat, secretly I'm awfully proud of myself. I did it.

And the voice? Strangely, eerily, utterly silent. For the moment. I can hear nothing. Any thoughts I have on the subject seem to be my own. I think about smoking but I don't do it. I crave fags but won't have one. Pathetic.

I think about smoking but I don't do it

And how have the four years been? Troubled, dangerous, close to the edge. I have grown fat – put on about two stone, but that is on top of the two stone over the two stone over weight I was. Yep, you read that right. I need to lose six stone now to be back to where I should be. Long struggle and without a fag an impossible one. I'm busy practising being cuddly and funny. Everyone loves a fat, cuddly, funny man, don't they?

So, I'm still not smoking. It does get easier. I get fatter. I am very tense and now I don't drink real coffee either – it apparently makes me quite unpleasant with the children – so I have been switched to decaf. No fags. No coffee. Wonder what'll be cut off next. I have realised that the nicotine addiction was under control fairly early on but the emotional addiction is still very strong. I see some cool young hoodie smoking a rollup and I'm immediately jealous. I too want to be that young, that cool, that rebellious. Instead I've taken to fast red sports cars – how sad can you get? And I've realised I'm not going to live forever. I did think that once I had given up smoking I would live forever.

Y'know the sort of advertising they throw at you – 'If you smoke you are going to die' – well I figured that once I'd given it up I was going to live forever. But now I realise that something else is going to get me. I wonder what. And if I get told in advance – Y'know the sort of thing "Well, Mr Craze, you've got three months to live" – well, at least I could have a ciggie with impunity. But seriously I am glad I have given it up, glad I don't have to explain to my children what I'm doing, glad I don't have to keep leaping on and off trains at every station, glad I don't have to go outside on cold, wet evenings at friends' houses, glad my lungs don't hurt when I wake up in the morning, glad my clothes don't stink any more, glad my teeth are getting whiter again, glad I have done it. No, really glad. I know I'll always be a smoker but I am really, really glad I kicked it....for the time being anyway.

I am older, wiser, fatter – but at least I'm not smoking. At least I stopped smoking and stayed cool.

Just biding my time, matey, just sitting here biding my time......

"What do you think smokers would do if they didn't smoke? You get pleasure from it, and you get some other beneficial things, such as relief. Maybe you'd beat your wife."

New York Times Magazine, June 21, 1998 quoting a senior CEO and Chairman of a very large tobacco corporation.

Out of Your Townie Mind

Extract

Playing host to townie friends

The dream

They motor down on a Friday evening and arrive around supper time. You are so pleased to see them and they come in to smiles and hugs and a decent bottle or two of red warming next to the Aga. Over supper you regale them with tales of your move and how you've settled in and everything that's happened to you since you moved. Their stories of city life seem pale and boring in comparison to yours.

The next day you take them on a tour of the local attractions and they talk of making the move themselves. By Sunday lunch, which is very long and lingering, they are serious and asking you to send them the local papers so they can look for houses near you. Late Sunday afternoon you wave them off and, as they motor back to the city, you settle back to have a look at the papers and sip a last glass or two. There's nothing to do as your delightful guests loaded the dishwasher before they left, made their beds and emptied the ashtrays. They were easy to have around, great company and you're looking forward to them coming again.

The reality

If it is like that sometimes you will be lucky. Mostly you can't wait for them to go. They leave a bloody mess behind that takes you until Tuesday to clear up. When you knew your friends in the city you invariably met up with them for an evening. But the whole point about townie friends once you've moved to the country is that they stay for a whole weekend at a time. Suddenly you get to see them first thing in the morning…not pleasant. They have some very unsociable habits.

They arrive with kids and dogs and au pairs that you didn't know were coming. They suddenly seem very picky and faddy about food. They smoke in the bedroom. They insist on seeing all the local tourist attractions which you've seen every weekend since you moved. They mock you about moving to the sticks, instead of being suitably impressed. They seem bright and fun and young and you realise that living in the country has made you old fashioned, out of touch and drab. They won't go and are still there eating and drinking you out of house and home on Wednesday. You won't see them in the winter. They think you're a free B&B.

They say they'll turn up on Friday evening in time for supper but they actually arrive in the early hours of Saturday, crashing drunk, waking the kids and claiming the trains were delayed. Talking of trains, you spend the whole weekend driving them everywhere if they do come by train. God, weekend visitors are a nightmare. Entertain them? Yeah, sure, at first you might but you won't see them after a few visits. Or if you do they'll be a pain. They'll poke your fire and complain about how cold it is. They don't bring jumpers or wellies and expect you to provide them. They bring white and drink red – unforgivable. In fact, they bring cheap white and drink expensive red – even more unforgivable. They drink rather more of the expensive reds than you'd have thought possible.

The fact is that townie friends whom you used to socialise with for an evening will descend on you for a couple of days or more at a time. Sometimes several of them at a time. It's hard work, cooking every meal for several people for a weekend, preparing the beds, getting the shopping in, tidying up (at least a bit) and putting off your usual weekend activities.

Once they've arrived, you find your privacy is severely curtailed for 48 hours or so rather than just an evening, and you feel obliged to stay up every night until they want to go to bed, and be up in time to get them breakfast in the morning. We all have different styles of entertaining, but however laid back you are, weekend guests put paid to any ideas of a relaxing weekend for you. You'll be too busy giving them a relaxing weekend.

And it's expensive. A weekend shopping bill when you have friends staying – especially when you want to give them a good country weekend with a Sunday roast and plenty of apple pie and home cooking – can come to as much as your usual weekly shop when you're on your own.

You'll soon find that while some friends are always welcome, others quickly get to be a pain. They become boring after the first few hours, but you're stuck with them for another two days, and they simply don't pull their weight so you have endless clearing up to do after them. And then there are the ones who eat all your food and then disappear for the day, returning only for a slap-up supper at your expense. They just wanted a free weekend in the country, with all meals cooked and washing up done for them. You come to dread them visiting.

And, you see, there's a funny thing. People don't wait to be invited for a weekend in the country. The etiquette seems to be that they phone up and invite themselves to stay. I sometimes wonder if it isn't due to a feeling that they're doing you a favour – deigning to keep you in touch with civilisation. Saying no politely can be tricky, too, because they often ask, "When would be a good weekend for you?" Either you have to be rude, or you have to let them come.

Apparently Malcolm Muggeridge used to tell of a time he and his wife stayed with friends for the weekend. They drove away after having said their farewells when Muggeridge remembered they'd left their umbrella in the front porch. Rather than disturb their friends his wife popped back to collect it and was startled to see, through the glass porch, their hosts in their sitting room doing a bizarre little dance which involved hopping from one foot to the other while waving their arms in the air and chanting 'they've gone, they've gone, they've gone, they've gone'.

Of course it's not always like this. Some friends will be an absolute delight and will clear up after themselves and be entertaining, helpful, friendly, suitably awed about your move, interested in what you are doing and it's brilliant to catch up on all the gossip. They offer to walk your dogs for you, look after your kids so you can have a nap after cooking that huge Sunday lunch, bring a decent red and some flowers, get a taxi back to the station after lunch and drop you a note to say thanks later in the week. That's perfection. If only it happened more often.

Pros

- The best guests are a delight, and it's a treat to see them for a whole weekend instead of just for an evening.
- It's great fun when friends visit your country house, applaud you for making the move, and admire your garden, your home, your surroundings and all the rest of it.
- You can't beat a long, lazy Sunday lunch in the country, whether it's outdoors in the summer or in a steamy Aga-warm kitchen in winter.

Cons

- Until you're subjected to your friends for 48 hours at a time, you can't always be sure which ones are still fun after two days continuously in their company.

- It's hard work having weekend guests.
- It's very expensive entertaining people in the style to which you would like them to think you have become accustomed.
- Townies rarely have guests to stay over (except maybe crashing on the sofa when they've missed their last train home and are too drunk to ring for a taxi). This means they have no idea how much trouble they can be, so many of them fail to help with the cooking or washing up, leave a mess everywhere, bring extra children or dogs without warning, and don't contribute to the cost.
- People will happily invite themselves to stay for a whole weekend, making it quite hard to avoid unwanted friends politely.
- Some people find the lack of privacy and time to yourself, that goes with having people in your house for days at a time, difficult to cope with.
- Some guests, quite frankly, exploit and abuse you, using you as a free B&B.
- Even those who don't abuse you will still choose to visit in good weather, quite understandably. You may not see any of your townie friends all winter.

Key questions

- Are you used to having people stay for two or three days at a time? Do you know how much work is involved?
- How laid back are you about mess, clean sheets, smoking in bedrooms, leaving the washing up until morning and so on? The more particular you are about having things done your way, the more stressful you will find townie visitors.
- Are you happy to have a house full for days on end, or do you miss your privacy?
- Are you flush enough to keep paying for townie visitors? Some will contribute but others won't. Either way it will still cost you more than a weekend without visitors.

- How do you feel about being taken for granted/taken for a ride/exploited and abused? Is it worth it to see your friends? Or are you a happy martyr? Or will it frustrate and anger you?
- How assertive are you? To make this work, you may need to be firm about house rules, or even tell certain people that you don't want them to visit overnight.
- You can't stop people inviting themselves to stay, and you want to keep in touch with your friends. But if this aspect of country living doesn't appeal to you, would you be better off staying close enough to the city that friends can visit for the day rather than a whole weekend at a time?